THE CIVIL WAR DIARY OF
GENERAL JOSIAH GORGAS

JOSIAH GORGAS IN CONFEDERATE UNIFORM

Courtesy Mrs. W. D. Wrightson, Chevy Chase, Maryland

THE CIVIL WAR
★ ★ ★ ★ DIARY

of General Josiah Gorgas

Edited by *FRANK E. VANDIVER*

University, Alabama
UNIVERSITY OF ALABAMA PRESS
1947

Foreword

SOME YEARS AGO, AT THE AGE OF FOURTEEN OR SO, THE
editor of this document came under the influence of the
writings of Professor Charles W. Ramsdell, of the University of Texas. By the advice of that great scholar, and
to some extent under his direction, his particular interest
was turned to problems of supplying the Confederate
armies. In this field the fundamental problem was that of
ordnance, the task of providing an adequate supply of arms
and munitions with which to fight. Thus Mr. Vandiver's
studies quickly led him to Josiah Gorgas, the sober, un-
flustered gentleman whose success in building the efficient
Confederate ordnance service was little short of the difficulty of making bricks without straw.

Born in Pennsylvania, a graduate of West Point in the
class of 1841, and twenty years an officer in the United
States army, Gorgas nevertheless resigned on April 3,
1861, and five days later became chief of ordnance in the
Confederate army with the rank of major. He passed
through the successive grades and in November, 1864, was
promoted to the rank of brigadier-general by the interces-
sion of President Davis, who appreciated his supreme
efficiency.

Though a copy of the diary has been accessible to
scholars in the Library of Congress, publication previously
has not been allowed, and permission to publish now is, in
large measure, a tribute to the industry of the young editor.
As a sidelight on life in Richmond during four years of
war and a comprehensive personal commentary on military

v

112867

events, the diary is interesting and valuable. General Gorgas knew many officers in both armies and his comments on their performances are often pointed and enlightening. Except in his own department, however, he seems to have had access only to the public sources of information and his writings contribute little, therefore, to the factual history of the war. Even in the field in which he was so eminently the master, factual entries probably do not exceed a dozen, confined to casual comments on blockade runners and importations from abroad.

Happily, disappointment over his reticence is lessened by information that Mr. Vandiver is working on a biography of General Gorgas and that he is soon to publish the letter books of Confederate agents covering importations from Bermuda.

EUGENE C. BARKER

The University of Texas,
Austin, April 20, 1947.

Preface

MEN AND WOMEN KEEP DIARIES FOR VARIOUS PURPOSES—
some for personal gratification, some hoping for future
publication, and some as memory aids. Josiah Gorgas,
Chief of Ordnance of the Confederate Army throughout
the Civil War, wrote for his family's enjoyment. Beginning
it in 1857, nearly three years after the birth of his eldest
son, William Crawford, of Panama Canal fame, Josiah
Gorgas kept a well-sustained journal, mainly as a guide
for Willie as he grew up. In certain respects the journal
more resembles a chronicle of contemporary events than a
diary, for it records comparatively little of the daily activity
of the writer, and much of the happenings in the world
around him.

Though the journal covers the period between January
1, 1857, and July 1, 1877, only the section through the years
1861-1865 is printed here. The version here reproduced follows a typescript copy made from the original diary, kept
in small note-books, under the direction of William Gorgas.
Exactly when this transcript was made is not certain. The
typed copy has been checked against the original and found
to be reasonably accurate. The editor has divided the diary
into chapters and supplied the headings. Some deletions
have been made at the request of the Gorgas family.

It is difficult to determine arbitrarily the chief value
of Gorgas's diary as a historical document. It would be
erroneous to say that his account of various battles is its
greatest interest, or that his discussion of living conditions
in war-torn Richmond is the most important information

it contains. John B. Jones, in his *Rebel War Clerk's Diary*, has covered living conditions in Richmond, and many other writers have given descriptions of battles. From Gorgas's position as Chief of Ordnance of the Southern Army, one would naturally expect the crux of his journal to lie in his discussion of Confederate Ordnance. But such is not the case, and the reason is obvious. The importance of his bureau made it unwise from the standpoint of military security to commit any information concerning it to writing.

It would appear, perhaps, that the greatest value of Gorgas's diary lies in what he reveals of himself, even while writing of other things. In general he was looked upon as austere and even grim, and his wartime photograph tends to support this impression. His diary, on the contrary, shows him as an affectionate husband and father, a man of deep feeling. His personal likes and dislikes appear clearly as does his complete faith in the success of the Confederate cause.

In final analysis, the diary's greatest worth may lie in the insight it affords to the personal attitude of Gorgas on the questions affecting the prosecution of the war; his feeling toward his close personal friend, Jefferson Davis, and his opinions of many of the Confederate hierarchy.

The eminent position he held in the Confederate government gives peculiar significance to his views on problems facing the Confederacy. Appointed Chief of Ordnance with the rank of major on April 8, 1861, he rose through the grades to brigadier-general on November 19, 1864. Beginning with little or nothing in matter of ordnance stores, Gorgas doggedly set out to make the South industrially able to defend herself. The problems he faced were almost insurmountable, yet his unrelaxed efforts succeeded so well in importing arms from abroad, setting up arsenals, armories and factories, in building a national powder works and several rolling mills, and in fostering the cultivation and exploitation of the South's mineral and ore deposits, that at no time, after the crucial first year, was there a serious shortage of ordnance supplies. The Ordnance Department, unlike the Confederate Quartermaster and Commissary Departments, was able to meet the requisitions coming from all parts of the South.

/General Gorgas has long been regarded as the administrative genius of the Confederacy,'and as one of the ablest officers in the Southern Army. The products of his industry had profound influence on the course of the war: they went with Lee to "the farthest point North," and with H. H. Sibley to Santa Fe. Without them, the Confederate States would have been short-lived indeed. It required more than ability, genius in fact, to devise substitutes for leather, fulminate of mercury, and copper; to find new sources of such scarce items as nitre, lead and sulphur; to contend successfully with dilapidated railroads and move supplies and equipment to the front in adequate quantity and in time. Above all, it required keen discrimination to select subordinates with ability to devise the substitutes and seek out scarce and necessary supplies—subordinates of the calibre of Colonel John William Mallet, F. R. S., Superintendent of Confederate Laboratories, Colonel James H. Burton, builder of the English Enfield Works, Superintendent of Confederate Armories, and Colonel George Washington Rains, builder and commandant of the Government Powder Works at Augusta, Georgia.

"Mamma" of this diary was Amelia Gayle Gorgas, the daughter of Governor John Gayle of Alabama. She was married to Josiah in 1853, while he was commanding Mount Vernon Arsenal in that State. They had six children—two boys, Willie and Richard, and four girls, Jessie, Mary Gayle, Christine Amelia and Maria Bayne. "Hugh" of the diary was Hugh Aiken, husband of Amelia Gorgas's sister, Mary. "Bayne" was Thomas L. Bayne, in charge of the Confederate Bureau of Foreign Supplies. He was the husband of Maria Gayle, a sister-in-law of Josiah.

Josiah, himself, was born in Lancaster County, Pennsylvania, on July 1, 1818. The youngest of ten children, he had no easy time obtaining an education, but he finally secured an appointment to West Point. He entered the Military Academy in 1837 and was graduated sixth in the class of 1841 with an assignment to the Ordnance Corps. After travelling abroad on leave during 1845 and 1846, he returned home in time to participate in the Mexican War, serving as commander of the United States Ordnance Depot at Vera Cruz during most of the time from 1846 to 1848. From 1848 to 1861 he lived the routine life of an army officer, commanding various arsenals in the North and South. In February, 1861, while commanding Frankford Arsenal at Philadelphia, Pennsylvania, he was offered a commission in the embryo Confederate Army organizing at Montgomery, Alabama. After agonizing deliberation, he accepted, at the cost of severing his ties with his brothers, sisters and northern friends. He resigned from the United States Army on April 3, 1861. The part of the diary here published takes up the story from that point and carries it to May 14, 1865. After the war, Gorgas tried to resuscitate the moribund Brierfield Iron Works, near Ashby, Alabama, but failed. In 1869, he joined the staff of the University of the South at Sewanee, Tennessee, in time becoming its Vice-Chancellor. In 1878, he resigned this post to accept the presidency of the University of Alabama, a position he retained for about a year, until failing health forced him to assume the lighter duties of librarian. He died at Tuscaloosa, Alabama, on May 15, 1883.

The editor wishes to thank Miss Maria Bayne Gorgas and Mrs. George Palfrey, daughters of General Gorgas, and owners of the original diary, for the privilege of printing it, and for their unfailing kindness and help. He wishes to thank also Mrs. William D. Wrightson and Mrs. Jessie Leake, granddaughters of General Gorgas, for similar favors.

He desires to express his heartfelt appreciation of great kindnesses received from Dr. Douglas Southall Freeman,

Dr. Walter Prescott Webb, Dr. Eugene Campbell Barker, Dr. Ellis Merton Coulter and Miss Fannie Ratchford.

In conclusion, the editor would gratefully acknowledge his indebtedness to the Rockefeller Foundation for granting him a fellowship, which made the work on this diary possible.

FRANK E. VANDIVER

Austin, Texas
August 12, 1946.

Contents

1 ★ ★ ★

Richmond Hears The Cannons

Richmond, Va., June 12, 1862. Since the last entry in this journal I have passed the most eventful period of my life. Days appear like weeks, and the last day above entered confounds itself with my early life.

On the 7th of April [1861] I reached Montgomery, and, on the 8th, took charge of the Ordnance Bureau, being assigned to duty as Chief of Ordnance. On the 1st of June the government established itself here as being nearer the scenes of its most active duties. On the 10th of June was fought the first battle of the war, at Bethel,[1] near Yorktown. The Yankees were signally defeated, with heavy loss, while, on our side, was only one man killed. The artillery did excellent service. General Magruder[2] commanded our troops. A short time before this a man by the name of Jackson killed Ellsworth,[3] Colonel of Zouaves, for entering his home and attempting to haul down the Confederate flag on his house in Alexandria. Jackson was, of course, instantly butchered. His devotion had an electric effect, and was looked on as a happy omen of the spirit of the war. About the middle of July we suffered a reverse in western Virginia. General Garnett,[4] (a classmate), was killed and about four hundred of our men captured. This little success achieved with overwhelming numbers was the sole foundation of McClellan's[5] elevation to command subsequently.

On the 21st of July (Sunday) was fought the decisive battle of Manassas, or Bull Run.[6] It was preceded by a creditable affair on the 18th. The battle was fought by the united forces of Johnston, bro't from Winchester, and of Beauregard, the latter having made the disposition of the troops, before Johnston arrived. McDowell commanded the Yankees. The odds were very heavily against us, about 25,000 to 45 or 50,000. We routed the enemy completely, capturing twenty-eight pieces of artillery and a large number of small arms and stores of various kinds. Unfortunately the victory was not followed up, or Washington would have fallen into our hands without further contest.

About this time we heard of the victory at Springfield, Mo., which resulted in the death of Lyon,[7] (my classmate and roommate) and the retreat of his forces. Lyon was one of the most valuable of their Generals, being a man of more than average ability, and of unswerving purpose. He *would* have been the general of the abolition school! He was a man of cruel disposition, who would never forego an advantage over an enemy. He was the grandson of Col. Knowllon, an officer of the Revolution, from Connecticut. His ability was shown at West Point, chiefly in mathematics. He could not acquire languages, chemistry, or anything in which memory played a part.

Garnett, mentioned above, was a dashing man, and ambitious. He would have played a good part, and made an active enterprising general. His death was a loss. His capacity was very moderate as a scholar, but he had studied men and manners. He was the nephew of R. M. T. Hunter of Virginia.[8]

(I omitted to mention in its proper place that the bombardment of Fort Sumter, which began the war, took place on the 12th (Friday).[9] This began the war. Lincoln immediately called out 75,000 men, whereupon Virginia seceded, accompanied by Arkansas and Tennessee).

Up to this time and until the affair in Missouri, where we captured over a thousand prisoners, our success was uniform. In October our reverses began with the capture of Hatteras. Port Royal followed at no long interval—and early in this year, Roanoke Island; a sad blunder, where we lost 2500 prisoners. Then came Crittenden's disaster on the upper Cumberland,* relieved, however, soon after by

*Mill Spring.

our success at Belmont, opposite Columbus, Ky. But the chief of our reverses was the fall of Fort Donelson and the capture of its entire garrison and the army, then about 7,000 men. This, with the loss of Fort Henry, a week before,[10] opened the Cumberland and Tennessee to the gunboats of the enemy, and lost to us the state of Tennessee. Johnston fell back from Nashville to the line of the Memphis and Charleston Railroad, and the boats of the enemy ascended at once to Florence in Alabama, the river being very full. This was the great mistake of the War. Ten thousand men would have converted Donelson from an overwhelming disaster to a victory—and 18,000 men were literally doing nothing under Gen. Bragg at Pensacola and Mobile. If Grant had been beaten at Donelson, as he might easily have been with proper disposition of troops, the tide would have been rolled back into Kentucky. Our President is unfortunately no military genius, and could not see the relative value of position. Pensacola was nothing compared to Donelson.

The Missourians, under Van Dorn, fought about this time a bloody combat at Pea Ridge,[11] in which McCulloch[12] and McIntosh[13] were killed. It was indecisive but by no means discreditable to us.

On the 6th of April (Sunday) Johnston attacked Grant at Shiloh,[14] on the Tennessee, where he had effected a landing, and established himself. The forces were not very equal, Grant having heavy divisions of which four were engaged. He was drawn completely from his camps, back to the river under the fire of his boats, and darkness found him completely defeated, our troops being everywhere in possession of their camps. During the night the advance of Bull's[15] Column arrived, on the other side of the river, and began crossing. The fight was renewed next day, and our troops gradually forced back again, without confusion however. Unfortunately Johnston fell on Sunday at about 2:30 p.m., and Beauregard was left in command. Had Johnston continued in command it is possible that his genius and energy would have crushed Grant before night bro't darkness and Bull to his rescue. The loss was heavy on both sides. Neither party in this contest appear to pay much regard to truth, and especially in the statement of losses must accounts be read with caution. Our loss was probably 5,000,* while the enemy lost a few thousand more.

After the fall of Fort Donelson our forces evacuated the lines they had held since last summer at Manassas; all the Potomac was abandoned, and our troops fell back, first to the Rappahannock, and very soon were transferred to Yorktown, whither McClellan had transferred his force. The lines at Yorktown were held until some time in April when the Army fell back to Richmond. On the retreat was fought the bloody combat of Williamsburg, of which we had the best.

The abandonment of Yorktown and the Peninsula it is said necessitated the evacuation of Norfolk, and with it came the destruction of the "Merrimac" which had produced such terror in the Yankee Navy.

About the 10th of March she attacked the whole Federal Squadron in Hampton Roads. With her iron prow she ran into and sank the Cumberland in five minutes. She then attacked and destroyed the "Congress," both of them frigates of the largest class. An ironclad vessel called the "Monitor" armed with two heavy guns in a revolving tower, which had just come down from New York, interposed and saved the whole fleet from destruction. Com. Buchanan, the commander of the "Merrimac" was wounded.

No one event of the war, not even the disaster of Fort Donelson, created such a profound sensation as the destruction of this noble ship. It was intended to bring her up the James River as far as her draught would permit after the evacuation of Norfolk. For this purpose she was lightened by throwing her coal overboard; but after all had been taken out she could not pass the bar at the mouth of James River. She was now in a condition nearly defenceless. Her iron sheathing had come up to the water line, and even

*More probably 12,000, while the enemy lost perhaps 15,000 and 3700 prisoners.

above it, and her fuel was gone; nothing was left but to
blow her up, which was done with 36,000 pounds of powder
on board.[16] It was indeed a fearful blunder, and one which
came very near being fatal to us. There was nothing now
to prevent the gunboats from reaching Richmond. The
battery at Drury's Bluff had but three guns mounted; the
obstructions were wholly incomplete, and the enemy could
have made their way right up to this city. Fortunately they
waited until a week after her destruction before making
the attempt. The obstructions were completed, and when
they did make the attempt on the 17th of May they were
signally defeated. It was the turning point in our fortunes.

McClellan having crossed a portion of his troops over
the Chickahominy, Johnston attacked the Divisions which
had crossed on Saturday the 31st of May. The enemy were
driven back out of his camps, eight or ten pieces of artillery
captured, several standards and about four hundred prisoners, not without severe loss. The commander in chief was
seriously wounded,[17] Gen. Rittengen[18] wounded and a prisoner, Gen. Hatran[19] killed, and many field officers killed
and wounded. Our loss was about 5,000 killed and wounded;
that of the enemy perhaps greater, as they confess about
that many. The fight was renewed on Sunday morning,
but the enemy had been reinforced, and the attack was
abandoned. The fight was therefore undecisive. It was,
however, a heavy check to the enemy. One of his divisions
was entirely destroyed—that of Gen. Carey. The enemy is
now building bridges over the Chickahominy, consolidating
his position and making some advance along the York River
Railroad.

Sunday, June 15th. General Stewart has just come in
from a brilliant foray against the enemy's communication.
He started from Hanover—went round their rear—destroyed two transports in the Punxautony [*sic*] cut up
several trains, and bro't in about 150 prisoners and 200 to
300 mules—without any loss.[20]

About the 1st of June and last of May General Jackson

succeeded in completely routing General Banks in the valley, and driving him across the Potomac. He has since retired up the valley, followed by Fremont and by Shields,
whom he has separately met and driven back with loss. In
a skirmish a week ago Gen. Ashley, a distinguished cavalry
officer, rather of the partisan kind, fell, greatly lamented.[21]
The loss of the enemy in their operations in the valley has
been very great. 3,000 prisoners were taken, and a large
amount of army stores, medicines, &c.

Monday, 16th. Some skirmishing took place yesterday,
and at one time a regiment of the enemy was in our toils,
but a very heavy storm came on and prevented the capture.
A captain and seven or eight prisoners only were taken.
The enemy is said to be pressing into East Tennessee, being
relieved from the pressure on their front by the retreat of
Beauregard from Corinth. It is a point of weakness to us
there where there is so much Union sentiment. A little
fight has taken place at Secessionville, on James Island
near Charleston, the enemy attacking and being repulsed
with the loss of forty prisoners. —Jackson saved himself
from capture the other day by great presence of mind. He
had crossed a bridge over the Shenandoah, with a couple
of aides and ridden to a hill at some distance. Coming back
he found the bridge in possession of the enemy and a piece
of artillery on it. He rode up to it at once, at full speed,
and ordered it to be placed in a different position. They took
him for one of their own officers and immediately "limbered
up" and moved off. He put spurs to his horse and rode
over. His aides were taken, but subsequently recaptured.[22]

Wednesday, 18th. The reconnaisance made by Stewart,
which resulted so brilliantly, was ordered by Lee, Com-
mander-in-Chief,—he should have credit for the orders. I
have seen the President today. He appears very much dis-
contented with Beauregard's movements at Corinth. They
are certainly inexplicable.

Friday [*20th*]. No results yet. A heavy skirmish took place on Wednesday, with some loss on both sides; how much on that of the enemy is not known, about sixty killed and wounded on our side. Exaggeration is so much indulged in by both sides that it is difficult to find the exact truth. The Yankees are probably the greatest liars, but we are not much behind hand. Much speculation is still indulged in as to the course of England and France in this war. How much evil they could have spared to their own people and to us, had they acknowledged our independence, after the battle of Manassas when they could very properly have done so. I trust a new era is about to dawn upon us in the defence of our cities; and that no more will fall like New Orleans and Memphis, until they are captured by land forces. The evacuation of New Orleans by Lovell is a shameful chapter in our history. He should have insisted on the defence of the city and asked for 48 hours to remove the women and children.

Sunday, June 22nd. Preparations are evidently being made for a general action. Jackson with, I hope, 20,000 men is coming down from Gordonsmith[23] to fall on McClellan's right, I presume, while another attack is being made in front by our forces here. Another Sunday will see us either victors, and defiant, or beaten and humiliated. Your* mother and all the children, except yourself are at Greensboro, N. C., —you at Winsboro, S. C. All the little girls and baby Ria have measles, after having had them, as we supposed, last winter.

Tuesday, June 24th. There is very little firing along the lines. The battle may take place tomorrow or next day or the next or ten days hence, but probably cannot be long delayed. I think it may take place Thursday. A train leaves tomorrow morning for Hanover, where Gen. Jackson *may* be. It will carry ammunition which he needs, and therefore, he will not be ready tomorrow morning. I fear if there

*Willie.

is much delay Fremont and McDowell may unite and fall
upon Jackson before he can attack the right of McClellan's
army. Poor little Ria is still very ill, according to her
mother's letter of Sunday. I am very anxious about her.
She has measles and is teething.

Friday, June 27th. The great battle is now going on.[24]
It opened yesterday on our left, at about five p.m., perhaps
earlier, and continued until 9:30 p.m. At four this morning
the fire was resumed. It is now seven a.m. and going on
with vigor.

Saturday [June 28th]. Yesterday the enemy were driven
from their positions at Powhite Creek after a desperate
and bloody conflict. The ground is still covered with their
dead—in one field there are forty or fifty of the Zouaves
lying. They are being buried in trenches.—Just before I got
out today two regiments of Coomb's [Toombs'] brigade had
charged on a battery of the enemy on this side of the
Chickahominy, below New Bridge, and were repulsed with
heavy loss. It is said they took the battery but were unsup-
ported and could not hold it. I have had a long and severe
ride to the battle field of yesterday, and back.

Tuesday [July 1]. The enemy left his position on the
north bank of the Chickahominy and massed his troops
on the south side. On Sunday morning he began to abandon
his position on the south side, and took up his retreat for
the James River about Curley Neck, or Dutch Cap. Huger[25]
was negligent and permitted him to get away unperceived.
A vigorous pursuit was made at once by Longstreet's, Hill's
and Magruder's divisions—Jackson covering the Chickahominy behind McClellan and pressing on the left. There
was a good deal of fighting on Sunday and a very heavy
battle on Monday, the enemy showing a determined front.

Today has been the severest battle, tho' not so critical as
that of Friday. The enemy took post near the junction of
the Quaker and Darbytown Road, and, with his artillery,

mowed down our troops. Our loss was very severe. He withdrew toward the close of the fight, and during the night continued his retreat. I rode out and was within a mile of the field during the heat of the battle. The firing was very heavy; my ride of nearly thirty miles between 4:30 and 11:00 was fatiguing.

Friday, July 4th. There has been no more serious fighting since Tuesday. The enemy has reached the river and is resting under cover of his gunboats, below Turkey Island. He is committing ravages on the crops and stock of the vicinity. Whether there will be anything more done to molest him I know not. Prisoners are coming in daily; we have about 5,000, I suppose, and two generals—McCall[26] and Reynolds,[27] the latter of my class.

July 8th. The enemy has attained a comparatively safe position without much further loss. The word "safe" in this connection tells the full extent of his late reverses forcibly enough, and indicates the nature of our success. From a bold and threatening attitude he has been reduced to one which is characterized as "safe," that is the first tho't connected with it. He has been driven from Mechanicsville along the north bank of the Chickahominy, below New Bridge; across the Chickahominy and thro' the marshes and thickets of White Oak Swamp to the James River, at Herring Creek, where he now lies under cover of his gunboats. Where are now the brilliant hopes which centered in the possession of Richmond? McClellan was certain to be in Richmond; there was no doubt about it. He *was* six miles off *then*—*now* he is 25 miles away, having lost in the meantime not less than 25 to 30 thousand men, forty to fifty pieces of artillery—an immense amount of stores, wagons, and camp equipment of all sorts. We have about 5,000 well prisoners and 2,000 wounded ones, including two general officers.

The papers (one of them at least), grumble that McClel-

lan has "slipped thro' our fingers." We should have gladly
compromised for such a "situation" two weeks ago.

Mamma writes from Greensboro that Ria is still ailing
—poor little baby—the summer will go hard with her, and
I long for the cool days of October. The last three days have
been intolerably hot and I have been by no means well. I
have practised abstinence, however, and shall soon get right
again. I impress this important fact on Willie that with
his constitution a few days "fasting" is worth all the
medicine in the world. Whenever I feel ill I diet, and have
thus avoided the use of medicine almost entirely. I have
found a half grain of "blue mass," without anything else,
a very good corrective in warm weather. Sluggishness of
the liver seems inherent in my organization; at least I
cannot endure warm climates with impunity.

July 27th. I returned from Greensboro after an absence
of a week, on Wednesday. I found all well except Ria, who
was very ailing, and her poor little face looked pinched and
had a fixed expression of suffering. Mamma writes that
she is now, however, improving. I found them in a fine large
building—a Methodist college—with forty or fifty refugees.
The surroundings are very attractive, and the air very
salubrious. It stands on the outskirts of the little town which
has about 1500 inhabitants. On my way down I stopped at
Edenburgh to visit our lead smelting works there, under
charge of Dr. Piggott. To this point I rode in the conductor's
car on a trunk with Senator Orr of S. C. So full were the
cars with wounded soldiers and their friends that we could
not get seats. The railroads are badly conducted, and it is
impossible to get along with any degree of comfort. Baggage is no longer taken care of, and travelers must do the
best they can. The great struggle in which we are engaged
disorganizes everything which is not energetically super-
vised.

This month has been signalized by the defence of Vicksburgh, under Gen. Van Dorn, and by the operations of Col.
Morgan and Forrest, in Central Kentucky. Vicksburgh has

been bombarded heavily, without much injury, and the
enemy has been foiled by its determined occupation. He
cannot get command of the Mississippi, and has withdrawn
his forces. All his work to get command of the River is,
therefore, lost. Morgan and Forrest have taken and held
various towns and cities about Frankfort and Lexington,
and have burnt bridges on the road between Lexington
and Louisville.

Jackson's command has been sent up the road toward
Fredericksburgh and Gordonsville to hold Pope in check
and to defeat him if he attempts to move southward. The
day is beautiful, and the air pleasant. It is Sunday and I
attended church this morning. I omitted to state that Mamma and I were baptized and confirmed on the same day
(Tuesday, May 6, 1862). —President Davis and one other
person were the only others confirmed, the confirmation
being held by the bishop for him—Rev. Mr. Minnegerode[28]
baptized us in St. Paul's church. My mind has since turned
oftener toward religious tho'ts, and I trust I shall benefit
by thus linking myself to the visible church. —The death
of Gen. Twiggs[29] occurred about the middle of this month,
at an advanced age. —Bragg has succeeded Beauregard in
the command of the army in Miss., and is now moving on
Chattanooga by way of Mobile. He will, I believe, be able
to drive Buell back and perhaps redeem Tennessee, if not
Kentucky.

August 3rd. Troops have been moved in large numbers
up to re-inforce Jackson at Gordonsville. News of a battle
is expected from there and from Chattanooga, where our
troops are now face to face with the enemy; Bragg at C.,
and Jackson at Gordonsville. Buell opposes Bragg and Pope,
Jackson. Pope is morally worthless—Jackson is a just and
upright man, and in earnest. Providence will help the
righteous man who puts his shoulder to the wheel. Between
Bragg and Buell there is little to choose on the score of
morality. On Thursday night our siege and field guns attacked the transports of the enemy in James River, at

Coggins Point, after midnight. What damage was done does
not appear. Night attacks are seldom worth the trouble
they give. Mamma writes that she remains at Greensboro
as Ria is so much better.

August 8th. News was received yesterday of heavy fighting at Baton Rouge. General Breckinridge[30] attacked the
enemy and drove them toward the River until stopped by
the arsenal, (which was probably fortified). His own loss
severe. General Clark of Mississippi mortally wounded.
Gen. B had withdrawn his troops, to renew the attack in
half an hour. Three or four thousand of our prisoners arrived yesterday under the system of exchange, among them
Generals Buckner[31] and Tilghman[32]—the former was kept
in close confinement for $4\frac{1}{2}$ months.

August 9th. Three divisions (at least) marched down
to Malvern Hill on Wednesday to confront 20,000 of the
enemy. The troops lay in front of the enemy all night expecting to attack in the morning. But with the morning
the Yankees had vanished, and our troops marched back.
A bulletin says that we have captured Morgan's forces at
Cumberland Gap—too good to be true. This Morgan came
to West Point just as I graduated—then a full grown man,
and it was said having already fought with the Texans
against Mexico. He stayed there but a few months (or
less). I next saw him as Colonel of a regiment in Mexico.
I shall be glad to meet him a third time as a prisoner. No
further news from Breckinridge, and it is feared that he
was roughly handled at Baton Rouge. An unpleasant
rumor says the "Arkansas" (ram) had to be blown up, her
machinery having given out, and she became unmanageable.

Gen. Stewart [Stuart] sent in over 100 prisoners, and
about the same number were taken at Malvern Hill. —The
weather is the hottest I have yet felt here. —(The destruction of the "Arkansas" is confirmed. Her machinery became deranged on her passage down the river. She was run

ashore for repairs, and, while in this situation, was attacked by the enemy's fleet).[33]

August 11th. Troops moved yesterday to join Jackson, who it is said captured a General and other officers. As an order has been issued that, in consequence of General Pope's conduct toward citizens, the officers of his army shall not be entitled to be considered prisoners of war, the capture of officers is looked to with peculiar interest. The brilliant passage of the "Arkansas" thro' the enemy's fleet three weeks ago, destroying several of them, made us hope much of her. Had she lived New Orleans might have been retaken. With her dies all hope of re-conquering the Mississippi. —Yesterday and Saturday were the hottest days I have felt here. In the afternoon a thunder shower cooled the air and laid the dust.

August 14th. General Lee has gone to take command of the army near Gordonsville, which now contains the greater part of the troops, Longstreet's Corp having been sent up. It will be necessary to drive the enemy out of Virginia before he can get his new levies into the field, which are to amount to six hundred thousand (600,000) men, viz: —300,000 militia called out for nine months, and 300,000 volunteers. If the Volunteers are not forthcoming by the 15th of August then a draft is to be made. A great tendency has been shown to avoid duty, an order has been promulgated permitting no one to go abroad. If we can but hold our own for the next nine months, of which I have no doubt, all will end well.

August 16th. From oppressive heat the weather has turned pleasantly cool. —General Lee called yesterday for the division of General Anderson, (R.H.),[34] and announced his intention to push forward beyond the Rapidan. The telegram was from Gordonsville. Mr. Lincoln would not receive the proclamation, or order of the President, ordering that Pope's officers should not be treated as prisoners of war, in consequence of Pope's infamous orders holding citizens responsible for the shooting of his men by guerillas, or rangers. Lincoln says it is an insult to his government. McClellan says that he is ordered by the Commander in Chief to say that the war will be conducted, on their side, according to the usages of civilized warfare. What a "coming down" for McClellan, to be obliged to confess himself "second," who was so late the Napoleon, the idol of the people and the Army. —Mamma writes that she is very comfortable and that the children are all well. She has not heard again from Willie, who has the whooping cough very lightly.

August 20th. McClellan has crossed the lower Chickahominy and moved over to the Pamunky [*sic*] to place himself in supporting distance of Burnside at Fredericksburg, eventually, no doubt. It seems to me our troops are very inert to allow him to make this movement without being harassed. The battle of Cedar Mountain, fought on Saturday, the 9th, was very creditable to our troops. The enemy confess to great loss. Pope as usual issues a lying dispatch claiming the success, tho' in faint terms. Our troops under Jackson, made the attack, on Bank's corps, which was very roughly handled. Congress met on Monday, and seems inclined to vigorous measures. Our expenses have thus far been under $350,000,000, which is wonderful, considering that we have had for a year between three and four hundred thousand men in the field.

September 7th. Great battles were fought on the 28th, 29th and 30th on the old battle grounds about Bull Run. The enemy were repulsed on the first two days and defeated on the last. We have taken thirty or forty pieces of artillery, a great many small arms, and more than 7,000 prisoners. The loss of the enemy is vastly greater than ours. On the 3rd the enemy also suffered a signal defeat at Richmond, in Kentucky, by General Kirby Smith; three or four thousand prisoners were taken. Great hopes are entertained

of the campaign in Kentucky. I fear the result of the far
advance of our troops toward Washington, unless the campaign can be prosecuted into Maryland, and the troops sub-
sisted there. The acquisition of arms in these battles will
be very important to us. —Hugh and Mr. Bayne came here
last week—the latter stays with me. Hugh came to get his
command of Partizan Rangers mustered in. —Mamma still
stays at Greensboro, but will soon go to Winnsboro and
thence return here, not to leave again, I trust, until the
capitol is moved from here farther south. Baby Ria is getting as fat as a little pig again, after her summer of illness.

September 14th. Our Army has crossed over into Maryland and is now, I hope, at Harrisburgh and on its way to
Philadelphia. We shall have to fight one more great battle
to defeat that army now at and about Washington, and then
the enemy will be completely prostrate at our feet. God
grant us this victory, not for vengeance but for peace—let
us trust in Him.—In Kentucky General Kirby Smith is probably on the bank of the Ohio. I trust Cincinnati is ours, or
will be soon. Our forces in Kentucky and in Maryland are
sufficient to overwhelm the foe and now is the time for
audacity. —Uncle Tom, now Capt. Bayne, went to Winnsboro on Friday and takes Mamma and all the children along
with him, from Greensboro. In three weeks now I shall be
a joyful man on seeing them all back around me. —I saw
General Pillow[35] on Friday, and looking very well. He has
lost property by the Yankees to the amount of $700,000.
—Yesterday morning I was called before the Committee on
Ordnance Stores (of the House). Mr. Conrad is Chairman.
My Department is in a very satisfactory condition, and the
Committee were well pleased with my account of affairs.

September 21st. Last Sunday our Army captured Harper's Ferry with 11,000 prisoners and a large amount of
stores. From six hundred to one thousand negroes were recaptured. Yesterday the people were disturbed by the accounts of a Philadelphia paper of the 18th, received by flag

of truce, to the effect that on the day before Harper's Ferry had been retaken, Jackson and Longstreet killed and 40,000 of our Army killed and captured! As we have a messenger with the flags who left there on Wednesday we may safely pronounce it a canard. Will the fruits of our victories be peace? That is the vital question. —On Tuesday it is known that there was heavy fighting, in which McClellan's army was driven back, but no details are known, except the death of General Garland, of Lynchburg.[36] Our army was massed at [Sharpsburg]—west of Fredericksburg [sic] city on Wednesday.[37] It is doubtless safe, and with Harper's Ferry in our hands we have a reliable base in case of disaster.

No late news from Kentucky except that the Kentuckians are rallying to us.

October 4th. Our Army is not far from Winchester. After the heavy battles of Sunday and Wednesday (Sept. 17th) it withdrew to the Virginia side of the Potomac carrying with it nearly all the wounded and all of its baggage and stores. Longstreet's division lost an ammunition train before the battle, which was the chief loss of material sustained. Four pieces of artillery were lost on Thursday from the Corps of Artillery. We heard that Colonel Wyatt Aiken, of the 7th S.C., was mortally wounded, but it turned out otherwise and he is recovering, tho' shot thro' the breast, the ball entering near the left nipple and coming out under the shoulder blade. Some apprehensions are entertained lest the enemy may make a dash on Richmond. We could not muster above 12,000 men at the very utmost for its defence. The yellow fever is making some ravages at Wilmington, for the first time for forty years. This must be due to the vessels running the blockade from the West Indies. —Lincoln has issued his proclamation liberating the slaves in all rebellious states after the 1st of January next. It is a document only to be noticed as showing the drift of opinion in the northern Government. It is opposed by many there. —Mamma is still in Winnsboro, S. C. A bill has just

passed both Houses making the Chief of Ordnance a Brig.-
General. I shall hail the day which returns me to my grade
of Lt. Colonel—and peace. —Capt. Bayne is on duty with
me and relieves me more than I conceived possible. The
best indication of the times at the North is that gold has
gone up to 123—a very ominous feature in their currency.
With us gold is 210, and even more, but it affects us very
little because we buy scarcely anything abroad. It affects
their trade vastly. And now everybody is buying gold, and
it will entirely disappear, and there will be but little left
to pay for their importations. Trade will be ruined, and
chaos will follow, unless the war ceases.

Editor's Notes

1 A skirmish was fought at Big Bethel, Virginia, June 10, 1861. The
Union forces, under Major-General B. F. Butler were defeated by a
small Confederate force under Colonel J. B. Magruder.

2 John Bankhead Magruder (August 15, 1810-February 18, 1871) was
born in Winchester, Virginia. He was graduated from West Point in
1830, a brevet second lieutenant of infantry. Made brigadier-general
in the Confederate Army after the affair at Big Bethel, he was promoted to Major-General in October of 1861. "Prince John," as he was
called, displayed vigor and ability in delaying General McClellan's
advance up the Virginia Peninsula, but in the Seven Day's Battles
around Richmond he was faltering and inefficient. He was sent to
the Trans-Mississippi Department, where he remained, and after the
surrender of that Department, joined the army of Maximilian in
Mexico. Allen Johnson and Dumas Malone, eds., *Dictionary of American Biography* (cited hereafter as *DAB*), XII, 204-05.

3 Colonel E. Elmer Ellsworth, twenty-four-year-old commander of
the 11th New York, or "First Fire Zouaves," was shot in the heart
by James T. Jackson, keeper of the Marshall House in Alexandria,
Virginia, on the morning of May 24, 1861. This act proved a stimulus
to Northern war sentiment. R. U. Johnson and C. C. Buel, eds.,
Battles and Leaders of the Civil War (cited hereafter as *B&L*), I,
179.

4 Robert Selden Garnett (December 16, 1819-July 13, 1861) was born
at "Champlain," Essex County, Virginia. He was graduated from
West Point in 1841 (Gorgas's class) and was commissioned second
lieutenant of artillery. Serving gallantly in the Mexican War, he
emerged with the rank of major. In 1855 he was sent to the North-
west where he commanded the Puget Sound and Yakima expeditions,

and remained on duty until he resigned his commission to enter the Confederate Army. Commissioned a brigadier-general of the Confederate Army, he was killed while conducting a masterly retreat of his forces near Carrick's Ford, Virginia. *DAB*, VII, 158-159.

5 Major-General George Brinton McClellan.

6 The Battle of Manassas, or Bull Run, was fought July 21, 1861, and resulted in the decisive repulse of the Union advance under Major-General Irvin McDowell, by the Confederate forces under Joseph E. Johnston and P. G. T. Beauregard.

7 Nathaniel Lyon (July 14, 1818-August 10, 1861) was born at Ashford, Connecticut. He entered West Point with Gorgas and was graduated in the same class. He served ably in the Mexican War and was made Captain in 1851. He was the author of a series of articles (1860-61) in the *Manhattan* (Kan.) *Express*, "wherein he bitterly condemned Douglas, called President Buchanan a 'blue-eyed old hypocrite,' and praised Lincoln and the Republican party." Made brigadier-general in supreme command of the Union forces in St. Louis (May 1861), he attacked the combined State and Confederate forces at Wilson's Creek, Missouri. Although seriously outnumbered, Lyon fought a stubborn action and was killed at the head of his troops. *DAB*, XI, 534-35.

8 Robert Mercer Taliaferro Hunter (April 21, 1809-July 18, 1887) was born in Essex County, Virginia. He was elected to the United States Senate in March 1847. Between 1850 and the Civil War he was outspoken in his defense of Southern interests, and reluctantly withdrew from the Senate on March 28, 1861. He served as Confederate Secretary of State, July 25, 1861 to February 18, 1862, and then became a member of the Confederate Senate. He remained in this position until the fall of the Confederacy. After the war he bent his efforts to save Virginia from the ravages of Radical Reconstruction. *DAB*, IX, 403-04.

9 Confederate forces under General P. G. T. Beauregard opened fire on Fort Sumter, South Carolina, on the morning of April 12, 1861. The fort was surrendered the evening of the thirteenth.

10 The two severest blows struck by the Union since the outbreak of the war were the capture of Forts Henry and Donelson, guardians of the Tennessee and Cumberland rivers, respectively. Henry fell on February 6, 1862, and Donelson ten days later. For an excellent discussion of conditions in the Confederacy in mid-1862, including a resume of reverses suffered, see Robert S. Henry, *The Story of the Confederacy*, pp. 77-124.

11 The Battle of Pea Ridge, or Elkhorn Tavern, Arkansas, was fought on March 6 and 7, 1862, between Union forces under Major-General S. R. Curtis and Confederate forces under Major-General Earl Van

Dorn, resulting in the defeat of the Confederates. For an excellent military discussion of this confused action, see *B&L*, I, 314-334.

[12] Ben McCulloch (November 11, 1811-March 7, 1862) was born in Rutherford County, Tennessee. He followed "Davey" Crockett to Texas and saw service in the Texan Army at San Jacinto. Serving with dash in the Mexican War, he emerged from that struggle a major and returned to his profession of surveying. In February 1861, he was in command of the Texas troops which received the surrender of the U. S. forces at San Antonio. Later, commissioned brigadier-general, he was assigned to Confederate troops in Arkansas and, under Sterling Price in Missouri, had the chief Confederate command at Wilson's Creek (August 10, 1861) and gained a victory. At the Battle of Elkhorn Tavern, near the beginning of the action, he was fatally wounded by a party of sharp-shooters. *DAB*, XII, 5-6.

[13] Brigadier-General James McIntosh, Confederate States Army, was killed at Elkhorn Tavern, March 7, 1862.

[14] The Battle of Shiloh, Tennessee, April 6 and 7, 1862, resulted, for all practical purposes, in a draw. The Confederates under veteran General Albert Sidney Johnston defeated U. S. Grant's Union army the first day, but, on the second day, Beauregard, commanding Confederate forces after Johnston's death on the 6th, was forced to withdraw. Grant did not pursue. Sources include: *B&L*; Stanley F. Horn, *The Army of Tennessee; Personal Memoirs of U. S. Grant;* Alfred Roman, *Military Operations of General Beauregard;* and Otto Eisenschiml, *The Story of Shiloh.*

[15] General Don Carlos Buell.

[16] The *Merrimac*, or *Virginia*, was blown up by the Confederates May 11, 1862, to prevent her falling into the hands of the enemy. For the reasons behind the destruction of the *Virginia*, see J. T. Scharf, *History of the Confederate States Navy*, p. 221.

[17] The Battle of Seven Pines was fought May 31 to June 1, 1862. Gorgas meant that General J. E. Johnston was wounded. General Lee succeeded Johnston in command of the Army as a consequence of the latter's being wounded.

[18] General "Rittengen" has not been identified.

[19] It is probable that Gorgas meant Major-General John F. Hartranft of the United States Army. General Hartranft was not killed.

[20] General J. E. B. Stuart made his famous "Ride around McClellan" June 11 to 14, 1862.

[21] Brigadier-General Turner Ashby (October 23, 1828-June 6, 1862) was killed at Harrisonburg, Virginia. He was a favorite with the

people. There was a poem written about him entitled "Dirge for Ashby." See Henry Kyd Douglas, *I Rode With Stonewall*, p. 77.

22 This undoubtedly is a reference to an incident which occurred on the morning of June 8, 1862, near the Kemper House, south of Port Republic, Virginia. Jackson mistook a company of Federal cavalry to be his own men and gave them orders. To his surprise, they wheeled and departed. See *ibid.*, p. 85.

23 Gordonsville, Virginia.

24 The Seven Day's Battles around Richmond, June 26 to July 1, 1862, major Confederate victories, resulted in the defeat of the Union forces under McClellan and their retreat from the vicinity of Richmond.

25 Benjamin Huger (November 22, 1805-December 7, 1877) was born at Charleston, South Carolina. He was graduated from West Point in 1825 and commissioned second lieutenant of artillery. He was Gorgas's immediate superior in the Mexican War and always held him in high regard. For gallant conduct during his service as General Winfield Scott's chief ordnance officer, Huger was brevetted colonel. Casting his lot with the Confederacy, he was made brigadier-general and later major-general. He was assigned as Inspector of Artillery and Ordnance, July 12, 1862. Later he was made chief of ordnance of the Trans-Mississippi Department where he continued until the war's end. On February 17, 1831, he married his cousin, Elizabeth Celestine Pinckney. Late in life he returned to Charleston, where he died. *DAB*, IX, 343; Mexican War Papers of Benjamin Huger, in the War Records Office, National Archives.

26 General George A. McCall, United States Army, was captured at the Battle of New Market Cross Roads, June 30, 1862, and was confined in Libby Prison from June 30 to August 16, 1862. See George W. Cullum, *Biographical Register of the Officers and Graduates of the United States Military Academy* (cited hereafter as *Cullum*), I, 293-94.

27 General John Fulton Reynolds (September 20, 1820-July 1, 1863) was born in Lancaster, Pennsylvania. He entered West Point the year that Gorgas entered and was graduated with him. Reynolds was captured at Gaine's Mill, June 28, 1862, and sent to Richmond. After six weeks in Libby Prison he was exchanged for General William Barksdale. Reynolds was killed in the first day's fighting at Gettysburg, July 1, 1863, while leading part of his command to the front. *DAB*, XV, 520-21.

28 Dr. Charles Minnegerode.

29 David Emanuel Twiggs (1790-July 15, 1862) was born in Richmond County, Georgia. He served in the War of 1812 and in the Mexican War. Commanding the Department of Texas, February 1861, he surrendered it, along with all the Union troops and supplies, to

General Ben McCulloch. For this action he was dismissed from the United States Army, but was commissioned a Major-General in the Confederate Army. He was too old actively to take the field. *DAB*, XIX, 83.

30 General John C. Breckinridge and his Confederates were repulsed in an effort to recapture Baton Rouge, Louisiana, August 5, 1862. Breckinridge was made Confederate Secretary of War in February, 1865.

31 Simon Bolivar Buckner (April 1, 1823-January 8, 1914) will be remembered for his surrender of Fort Donelson to General U. S. Grant. His fellow generals in the fort, John B. Floyd and Gideon J. Pillow, escaped, when this seemed impossible, and left Buckner in command. He hoped for terms from Grant on the basis of personal friendship, but was ultimately forced to surrender unconditionally. See *DAB*, III, 234-35; and S. F. Horn, *The Army of Tennessee*, p. 97.

32 This was probably Lloyd Tilghman. He was killed at Baker's Creek, May 16, 1863. *Cullum*, I, 659.

33 The *Arkansas* was blown up by her commander August 5, 1862, to prevent her falling into enemy hands. John T. Scharf, *History of the Confederate States Navy*, pp. 333-336.

34 R. H. Anderson's division was ordered to Lee, from Drewry's Bluff on August 15.

35 Gideon Johnson Pillow (June 8, 1806-October 8, 1878) was born in Williamson County, Tennessee. He was, for a time, a law partner of James K. Polk. He was one of Polk's political generals in the Mexican War, and was made a brigadier-general in the Confederate Army. He contrived to escape from Fort Donelson with General John B. Floyd and left Buckner in command. For a period following this flight, he was viewed with disfavor by Richmond, and was never subsequently given a command of any importance. *DAB*, VIV, 603-604.

36 Brigadier-General Samuel Garland was killed at South Mountain, Maryland, September 14, 1862, while leading his brigade. For a description of the manner in which he met death see Douglas S. Freeman, *Lee's Lieutenants*, II, 177.

37 Lee's Army, on the 19th, had begun the retreat to Virginia after the near disaster at Sharpsburg (Antietam), Maryland, September 17 and 18, 1862. See *ibid.*, pp. 203-25 for an excellent account of the Battle of Sharpsburg.

2 ★ ★ ★

The Army Reaches Gettysburg

October 17th [*1862*]. We are now anxiously expecting
news from Kentucky, where General Bragg has encountered
the forces under Buell, with doubtful result. The news from
our side is that we have captured guns and prisoners, and
achieved a decided success—but no one is satisfied of its
authenticity. Two weeks ago today our forces attacked the
enemy under General Rosecranz at Corinth, and were defeated.[1] General Van Dorn was evidently out-generaled,
allowing himself to be drawn into a trap, and getting his
forces very much cut up. Price commanded the Missouri
and other troops. The full details of the disaster are not yet
known but we have lost prisoners, arms and artillery. It
is a mournful result, risked without an object. The proclamation of Lincoln, freeing all slaves in "disloyal" states
after the 1st of January next, encounters marked opposition
at the north, and is denounced by the Democrats generally.
—Mamma is still at Winnsboro, with all the children, and
will not return until the first of next month.

Bayne and myself spent an evening at the President's
last week. He was very much depressed at the news from
Corinth, and said we had been out-generaled. —Mrs. Davis
was very talkative and inquired particularly about Mamma,
and said when we next "fled" from Richmond they would
go to Raleigh (where she had gone last May) together. She
is a lady of great good sense and of much more than
ordinary cultivation. . . .[2]

March 20, 1863. The five months which have elapsed
since my last entry have been fruitful in military events.
I regret that I have not entered them as they occurred and
can now only glance back over them. The battle of Perry-
ville closed the brilliant successes of the Kentucky campaign, by a drawn fight in which we captured artillery, and
inflicted heavy loss on the enemy. Bragg, however, effected
the object he had in view, viz: the withdrawal of the supplies he had captured. The military results of this campaign
were the capture of about 10,000 prisoners, eight or ten
thousand small arms, several batteries of artillery, and large
supplies of cloth and bacon for the Army. Bragg's forces
were now thrown on the road to Nashville and our pickets
approached within a few miles of the city. On the approach
of Rosecranz our Army fell back and took up a position a
few miles in advance of Murfreesboro' awaiting an attack.
Bragg threw himself vigorously on the enemy's right and
drove it back up his centre, inflicting heavy loss and capturing 3,000 prisoners and 27 pieces of artillery. This was
on the last day of the old year 1862. Had the fight stood
thus we should have had unchecked triumph. Unfortunately
Breckinridge attacked the centre and left of the enemy on
the 2nd of January and met with a bloody repulse, losing
full 3,000 men of his division and two pieces of artillery.
After this Bragg fell back slowly to Tullahoma where he
now is. The battle of Murfreesboro was fought with undoubtedly greatly inferior force, our Army numbering less
than 35,000 men; Rosecranz had probably 50,000 and over.
This great battle closed the campaign in middle Tennessee.
A series of brilliant cavalry dashes, under Wheeler and
Forrest, have, however, characterized the winter months.
These have resulted in the capture of a great number of
wagons, horses, &c., and the destruction of many more.
Among other exploits Wheeler attacked the transports of
the enemy below Nashville, at Cumberland Shoals, and sunk
one and destroyed several, with all their stores. The enemy
has thus been constantly harassed and a great deal crippled.

About the first of this month Van Dorn attacked and captured five regiments at Thompson's Station on the Columbia
Road, taking some 2500 prisoners, and killing and wounding many.

In North Mississippi Van Dorn pounced on the rear of
Grant's Army, at Holly Springs, some time in December,
and, besides taking many prisoners, destroyed stores to the
amount of it is said $10,000,000, which is perhaps an
exaggeration.[3]

At Vicksburgh the enemy attacked vigorously on the
Yazoo and were repulsed with heavy (Dec. 29) slaughter.
Several gunboats, the "Queen of the West" and the "Indianola," both ironclads, having passed the batteries at V.,
were captured by our enterprizing infantry. The "Queen
of the West" was used in the capture of the "Indianola,"
which vessel was sunk in nine feet of water and still lies
there.

About the 8th or 10th of this month the fleet of Farragut, from New Orleans, attacked Port Hudson and were
repulsed with the loss of the "Mississippi," burned by one
of our shells, and several of the larger sloops of war
crippled.[4]

The port of Galveston was also cleared of the enemy by
a daring attack on his ships, with cotton clad steamers,
which resulted in the capture of the "Harriet Lane" after
severe loss on board. Sabine Pass was soon after cleared
out and then the coast of Texas delivered of the enemy, and
the port of Galveston declared open—a declaration which
no one will heed. Thus the future of war in the West has
been largely in our favor, despite the capture of Arkansas
Post on the Arkansas, with about 3,000 prisoners, by the
land and naval forces of the enemy.

A few days after the achievement at Galveston Com.
Ingraham sallied out of Charleston with the two ironclads
under his command. He ran into the "Mercedita" cut a
hole into her and fired a seven inch rifle shot thro' her
boilers. She surrendered, her crew was paroled, but
eventually escaped as the ironclad had to follow other game.

Other of the enemy's vessels were also injured and the whole blockading fleet temporarily dispersed. The port of Charleston was declared open, but this too is disregarded, both by the enemy and by neutrals.[5]

On the Rappahannock the enemy under General Burnside[6] crossed the river at Fredericksburg and on the second day afterwards, Dec. 13, attacked our troops in position under General Lee. Jackson commanded our right wing and Longstreet our left. The attack was repulsed with great slaughter, and with little loss on our side, the loss being about 3,000 to 10,000. Generals Cobb and Gregg were killed on our side. Our Cavalry forces have been quite active, but with less signal successes than those achieved in Tennessee. After the defeat of Burnside, Gen. Hooker[7] was placed in command, and much is expected of him by the Yankees.

On Wednesday, the 18th, a cavalry force, said to be Averell's Division, crossed at Kelly's Ford, about twenty miles above Fredericksburgh, and drove in our pickets. They were handsomely defeated by the brigade of cavalry of General Fitzhugh Lee, and the battery of artillery attached to the brigade. Major Pelham[8] of Alabama, a very young and promising officer, was killed by a random shot. Major Puller[9] of Virginia was also killed.

Saturday, March 21st. Hood's Division which was ordered up on the report of the fight at Kelly's Ford, has returned to its position near Petersburgh. They marched back thro' a terrible snow storm. Our armies are increasing in size and will, I hope, be in good condition for the coming campaign.

A fearful accident occurred at our Laboratory here on Friday, the 13th of March, by which sixty-nine were killed and wounded, of whom sixty-two were females, chiefly girls and children. Only four were killed outright from the burns received in the burning of their clothes. The number of dead will probably reach fifty. It is terrible to think of— that so much suffering should arise from causes possibly within our control. The accident was caused by the ignition of a friction primer in the hands of a grown girl by the name of Mary Ryan. She lived three or four days and gave a clear account of the circumstances. The primer stuck in the varnishing board and she struck the board three times very hard on the table to drive out the primer. She says she was immediately blown up to the ceiling and on coming down was again blown up. Cartridges were being broken up temporarily in the same room, where many operators were sent temporarily on account of repairs in the shop they usually worked in. The deaths are due chiefly to the burning of their clothes.[10]

Mamma has been untiring in aiding, visiting and relieving these poor sufferers and has fatigued herself very much. She has done an infinite deal of good to these poor people.

Congress has for the past three weeks been engaged in secret session exclusively on the currency and tax bill. The former is too elaborate, I fear, *i.e.*, not simple enough; the latter is not yet announced. On these two measures will greatly depend the life of our young nation, as appears very evidently.

March 23rd. I spent an hour with the President at his office yesterday. He is at present evidently wholly devoted to the defence of the Mississippi, and thinks and talks of little else. I went to get some instructions as to sending ordnance west of the Mississippi. He read a long telegram from Pemberton, relating chiefly to the movements of the enemy, and expressing confidence in his ability to maintain the defence of the river. There is nothing special relative to the war; the conviction is fixing itself in the public mind that the end is not yet. The devastation the enemy commits is distressing. General Sparrow,[11] of Louisiana, Chairman of the Military Committee of the Senate, read to me a few evenings ago, an extract from a northern paper describing the present condition of his once beautiful place on Lake Providence, on the west bank of the Mississippi above Vicksburgh. It has been the headquarters of McArthur's[12]

Division of Yankees. Fences and outhouses are torn down for fuel, shrubbery destroyed, gardens and walks ruined, homes defaced and furniture dragged out and scattered about the camp. The family and servants have been removed. As the Yankee writer says, the place will shortly be restored to a wilderness. This is, of course, a faint picture of the actual state of ruin in this and many similar cases.

March 25th. Congress has, it is said, matured the tax bill and acted on it, but it is not yet announced. Every one prays that it may be one adequate to sustain the war and remedy the deplorable state of the currency. Gold is now at nearly five to one—provisions in proportion. Flour is $30.00 a barrel here, and twice and three times that price elsewhere. The difficulties of transportation add to the scarcity. We now pay three dollars per pound for butter; two dollars for eggs; a turkey costs fifteen dollars; beef is $1.50 per pound; common domestic is two dollars a yard; calicos are unobtainable. Of course in this state of things many colossal fortunes will be made. It is currently believed that the enterprizing firm of John Frazer and Company, at Charleston, have already made nine millions of dollars by importations. The manufacturing and business firm of the Crenshaw's[13] here are making out of woolen factories and flour contracts many hundreds of thousands monthly. But we salaried officers who do the work of the war are pinched. My pay will actually not purchase one thousand dollars' worth in ordinary times.

March 28th. We heard yesterday of a fresh attempt by the enemy to pass our batteries at Vicksburgh. Two boats attempted it—one was sunk with (probably) all on board; the other was apparently disabled and laid up at the mouth of the famous canal under cover of the batteries there.

Fast day was observed yesterday,[14] by going to church; but in my department work was carried on—laborare est orare. It will not do to omit anything now—we must both pray and work.

March 31st. The month goes out cooly but with a gleam of sunshine after a rainy morning. There is nothing of special interest. Pemberton telegraphs from Vicksburgh that the vessel sunk by our batteries a week ago was the "Lancaster," and the crippled one lying at the lower mouth of the canal is the "Monitor No. 2," built at St. Louis. —The tax bill does not seem to find general favor, and the remedy for our financial evils does not yet appear to be found.

April 2nd. There is a report said to be true that D. H. Hill had entered Washington, N. C., after a bloody combat, capturing a large number of negroes. It lacks confirmation, like many of our rumors. We also hear that our people made a successful dash at Ponchatoula, La., and took a good deal of property. —I met General Hood in the street yesterday and asked him to come to dinner. His Division had just been ordered below Petersburgh. It has been committing depredations in and about Manchester. Mamma entertained a few friends last evening, among them Mr. Barksdale,[15] M.C. from Mississippi; General Shoup,[16] who has been fighting under Hindman[17] in Arkansas. He told me a good deal about affairs in that Department. It is a lamentable record of bad management and of failures of the four considerable actions in Arkansas and Mississippi, viz:—Springfield, (where Lyon was killed) : Lexington, where the Yankee Colonel Mulligan and all his command were captured; Pearidge, or Elkhorn, and Prairie Grove. The first two were accidental victories and the last two disastrous retreats, if not positive defeats. —Major St. John,[18] my Chief of the Nitre and Mining Bureau, Lieutenant Ellicott of that Bureau, and Mrs. Guild, made up the guests. —Beef has now risen to $1.50 per pound and bacon to $1.60; butter is $3.50 to $4.00; eggs are $3.00, etc.

April 3rd. Yesterday a crowd of women assembled on the public square and marching thence down Main, sacked several shoe, grocery and other stores. Their pretence was

bread; but their motive really was license.[19] Few of them
have really felt want. The President went down amongst
them and said a few words to them telling them that the
course they were pursuing was the one most likely to bring
scarcity of food on the city. They soon separated and some
food was distributed. It was a real women's riot, but as yet
there is really little cause for one—there is scarcity, but
little want. Laborers earn $2.50 to $3.00 per day, and women
and children can earn $1.50 to $2.50. With such wages and
flour at even $30 they cannot starve. I spent an hour with
the President yesterday, talking over various matters,
especially the establishment of furnaces and a foundry on
Trinity River, in Texas. He understands the geography and
resources of the country very well. He spoke of the high
prices, and said that large as his salary appeared, and
altho' he lived just as he did as a Senator in Washington,
he found it took all of it to defray his expenses. No war
news. "Our" vessel, the "Cornubia," arrived at Wilmington
on Wednesday bringing 5200 arms and other stores.—Spent
the evening at Mrs. Jones,[20] on Sixth Street. Mr. J. thinks
the women ought to have been fired on, and augers badly
of the effect of their conduct on the markets.—The weather
was very fair yesterday, and promises well this morning.

April 4th. It is said today that the gunboats at Charleston have come up into Stono River, which bodes a land
attack, I suppose. The enemy seems to have failed in his
design of getting to the rear of Vicksburgh by Yazoo Pass.
—The bread riot demonstration has not been renewed. It
is denounced on all hands. There were few or no sufferers
in the crowd.—It is snowing furiously as I write at ten p.m.

April 6th. Nothing decisive has occurred at any of the
threatened points. General Sibley has captured a gunboat
on the Atchafalaya, with all on board.—Beyond the Rappahannock Capt. Mosby[21] has again captured a party of the
enemy, it is said. These accounts must be taken with al-
lowance on both sides. I find that our officers are nearly

as prone to exaggeration as the enemy.—From Mobile the only accounts relate dissipations of officers and society— an ungrateful picture to dwell on. From Florida it is said the Yankees have retired from Jacksonville with their negro regiments.—The enemy at Charleston was said to be on the Stono threatening a land attack.

April 7th. The next bulletin from Charleston is the great object of interest. Yesterday the enemy appeared off the bar with "24 wooden ships, the Ironsides, and six Monitors—two Monitors seem to be inside the bar—24 wooden vessels off Goat Island—fleet moving about all night." Perhaps the attack will develop itself today. Mosby's success is a fact, attested by the presence of the prisoners. The party was sent out to capture him! Meal is $16 per bushel yet there is no positive scarcity. I cannot fathom this state of things. I suppose the fear of scarcity combined with the plethora of money induces people to "lay up" a stock, and thus they enhance the price of provisions. Mr. Bujac and Mr. Seixas,[22] refugees from New Orleans, spent the evening. The former owned a large foundry and machine shop, and amused me, for he is no grumbler, with his narration of his flight from the city with such of his machinery as he could get off. The enemy's gunboat entered the dock he left about twenty minutes after his departure with his goods and chattels. He had some 1700 tons of iron, which would be of great value to us.

April 10th. On Tuesday, the 7th, at three p.m., nine iron-clads attacked Fort Sumter, at distances of about nine hundred to one thousand yards. After two to three hours firing they retired. One of them, the "Keokuk," is so damaged that she has sunk on the beach off Morris' Island. She is by no means the most powerfully armed, but was well clad with iron. She is 159 1-2 feet long, has two fixed turrets, is turtle or oval backed, and has two eleven inch guns. She is maneuvred with two independent screws. Was provided by Whitney.—In southwest Kentucky Pegram has met with a check,[23] having been driven back with loss from Somerset by forces under the Yankee General Gilmore (an old acquaintance).[24] It is now well established that the enemy is retiring from Vicksburgh.—Gold is again going up with great rapidity in New York. As it rises and falls with their prospects, it is esteemed an excellent barometer of their feelings on the war.

April 12th. The damage inflicted on Fort Sumter by the enemy's artillery without being serious is not to be despised. The Fort was struck about thirty-four times. Some of the indentations measure sixty inches in diameter and twenty-five inches in depth, which, in the parts between the tiers, where the wall is recessed for the gun and is only five feet thick, would soon make the casemate untenable. At a point where the hits are right over each other the wall may be said to be shaken. If thirty odd shots produce this effect what may be expected from one thousand, an amount readily fired from eight boats in ten hours. I have hopes that the covering of the lower tiers of guns by sand bags, laid eight feet thick, as directed by Colonel Gilmore, will greatly aid the resistance.[25] I believe, however, that a determined attack might be successful. The boats came up one at a time to the distance of nine hundred to twelve hundred yards, fired, and then gave place to another, so that only eighty shots were fired at the Fort in the two and a half hours of fighting. A gunboat was sunk on Wednesday in the Coosaw River, below Charleston, by field artillery.—No special news elsewhere.—The taking of the $15,000,000 Confederate loan in London is, perhaps, the most significant expression of foreign news yet given.[26] It is undoubtedly the forerunner of recognition. It was subscribed at 90, and rose immediately to five per cent premium. Of course the delivery of cotton, on which the loan is based, depends entirely on our ability to bring the war to a successful close; and the avidity with which the loan is taken up shows that this is a foregone conclusion among capitalists—the most cautious, and sensitive portion of the thinking public.

Dr. Spotswood and his son George spent the evening with us, and a Mrs. West Robinson came in to see me on business connected with a protegé of hers, whom the officers of his company wished to force back into the ranks. He is a clerk at the Arsenal. The conscription is rigidly enforced, and stragglers are pretty generally bro't back to their companies. System is being established in this vast army of 400,000 men, and it is getting to be manageable. —Monday evening we spent at Mrs. Jones', a beautiful and a very good woman, who took charge of all our children when Mamma was supposed to be lying at the point of death with scarlet fever, the last week of December '61. It was a winter of trial and sickness to me and mine. All the children had scarlet fever, and Mamma was convalescing.

Thursday, April 16th. We have rumors today that Suffolk has been taken by General Longstreet, with a large number of prisoners. A Yankee general is said to be slain. I doubt the story. Last week General Wise,[27] with about 1200 men, marched to Williamsburgh, and, sending troops to the rear, succeeded in inflicting some damage on the enemy, in destroying stores, wagons, and horses. No great results are ever hoped for when Wise heads any force, and, therefore, this little success is accepted in full of all promises. Wheeler is said to have again destroyed a gunboat on the Cumberland. He is very energetic and successful. He is a major-general, tho' scarcely twenty-three years old. No farther news of the ironclads at Charleston, which have left the harbor. The "Keokuk" is stated by Northern accounts to have been hit over one hundred times, of which ninety were near the water line.—Mamma, Bayne, and I have just returned from spending the evening at Gen. Randolph's,[28] late Secretary of War, where we drank good punch, ate some nice cheese, and met Mrs. Harrison, of Brandon, and Mr. Davis, Senator from North Carolina.[29]

Tuesday, April 21st. All rumors about operations at Suffolk were exaggerated. The object of the advance was simply to cover the country and draw supplies from it. That being accomplished our troops will probably fall back. D. H. Hill is still before Washington, N. C., and has alarmed the enemy for the safety of Foster. Did they know Hill as well as we do they would be little alarmed. He can never achieve a success, tho' he might, I suppose, blunder upon one, as other short-witted people do. Five or six more boats have lately run past Vicksburgh, so that there is now a fleet of eight under Farragut between Port Hudson and Vicksburgh. What their object is remains to be seen—probably marauding up the Red River.

The attack on Charleston seems to have been a confessed failure, and abandoned as such. The monitors were, it would seem, more seriously damaged than was at first supposed. No movement yet on the Rappahannock. The President has been quite ill for some days back.—Prices of provisions are coming down, people say, tho' they are still so high as to be nearly inaccessible. Beef has returned to one dollar.

Sunday, April 26th. No serious military event since my last entry. Hill has fallen back from Washington, but no great hopes were indulged of his success. So far as can be learned Longstreet still blockades Suffolk. His forces have contrived to lose a battery of five pieces (Capt. Stribling's),[30] among which are three Napoleons quite fresh from the foundry. The Yankees crossed the Nansemond below where the battery was placed and came up in rear of it—about 150 prisoners were made. They were marched thro' Suffolk, and were cheered by the women, who, they say, are not subdued tho' overpowered for the present. More gunboats and batteries have succeeded in passing Vicksburgh, and joining Farragut. With the heavy guns in position which are now on the way there, I hope the river will be of little use to them. Taylor,[31] we hear, is retreating from Opelusas, and that part of Louisiana, it is feared, is to be given up to the enemy including our Salt Works at Berwick. Our affairs west of the Mississippi have never prospered, probably because nearly all our means and attention were concentrated on the great theatres east. Perhaps the energy and ability of Kirby Smith will be felt before long in that department. Troops have been sent from Mobile into Tennessee where active operations are soon anticipated. The enemy abandoned Pensacola, burning and plundering several of the houses, about the middle of March, and confines himself in that quarter to Warrington. It has doubtless become necessary for them to concentrate detachments in order to keep up their main armies. Their nine months' and two years' men are to go home about the 1st of May, which, doubtless, weakens their force very materially. It is even doubtful whether they will be in force for aggressive operations before fall. This will be so far favorable that it will enable us to gather our troops without interruption. As food is a material question this will be an important feature in the operations of this year.

Thursday, April 30th. The news from the southwest is discouraging. Taylor has been forced back and has abandoned nearly all of Louisiana. The Salt Works are in the hands of the enemy and are destroyed. Alexandria if not now, will soon be in the hands of the enemy. Our troops have fallen back to Nackitoches [Natchitoches]. The enemy are reported to have crossed below Fredericksburg on Tuesday, on pontoon bridges, at Deep Run. This was the same place at which they crossed before. A heavy rain set in yesterday afternoon, and will doubtless delay the enemy. —Two vessels, the "Merrimac" and the "R. E. Lee" (Giraffe) have come in from Bermuda with stores for us. These vessels are running immediately under charge of the Ordnance Department. The first has three 170-pounder Blakeley guns; the second six thousand small arms and eight rifle pieces of good calibre.

May 2nd. Troops have crossed in considerable numbers at Deep Run and there has been some fighting. It is now said, however, that the main crossing is far up above Kelly's Ford, the point where the fight took place a month or more ago between the cavalry of the enemy and Gen. Fitzhugh Lee's brigade. Longstreet's corps is now moving up and will be in position in two days—or a part of it. This is all that is needed to insure the defeat of the enemy's plans, two divisions—Hood's and Pickett's—being down near Suffolk. The boats at Vicksburgh seem now to pass the batteries with comparative impunity. Lee's force, as I see by his return of arms, comprises about 50,000 infantry; the artillery and cavalry will carry it up to about sixty or sixty-two thousand—not over. With Longstreet's two absent divisions he will have nearly 80,000 effective men. Bragg had about the same number (60,000) but has been reinforced from Mobile and must have nearly 70,000 men. —Bayne went to Winnsboro yesterday, his little girl being very ill. I miss him very much in the office, and Mamma wants his pleasant company at home. He is always cheerful—an admirable constitution, unfortunately not my own.

May 3rd. There is no reliable news as to the operations yesterday, on General Lee's front. Rumors are rife and of course favorable, representing, for example, that Jackson had captured a brigade. Another report, not so favorable, is that the Yankees are continuing their course.—In the evening we received definite news of a Yankee cavalry raid which throws the whole city in violent commotion. A large cavalry force struck the central road at Louisa C. H. Having torn up the track it crossed and divided, one part continuing south toward the canal at Columbia; the other turning to the left, struck the Fredericksburgh road at Ashland, and captured a train of sick and wounded. Burning the cars, depot, etc., and tearing up a part of the track, the force, or a part of it, came down the Brooke Turnpike to within about four miles of the city. When this was known the utmost consternation prevailed in the city. All our troops had been sent off to Lee, and there were no guards in the batteries about the city. People were in utter despair, and even the Commanding General declared "we were ruined." Citizens (May 4) turned out with all sorts of arms and mustered on the public square. Senators and Cabinet officers fell into the ranks, and were marshalled to the batteries under direction of General Randolph.[32] The Yankees came no farther, however, but crossed over to the Central and finally to the York River Road, and were last heard of some ten miles off, making for the Peninsula. The party which struck for the Canal at Columbia, where there is an aqueduct, were overtaken by Fitzhugh Lee's Cavalry and driven back with some loss. So, happily ends the cavalry attack on Richmond. People were frightened and indignant, at such Yankee impudence.

May 5th. As the excitement of yesterday was dying away with the receding Yankees the city was cheered with the news of another great victory achieved by Lee over the forces of Hooker. It is announced by him in a dispatch bro't by courier, as follows: "To President Davis: today Gen. Jackson penetrated to the rear of the enemy and drove him from all his positions, from the Wilderness to within one mile of Chancellorsville. He was engaged at the same time in front by two of Longstreet's divisions. Many prisoners were taken, and the enemy's loss in killed and wounded is large. This morning the battle will be renewed. He was dislodged from all his positions around Chancellorsville and driven back towards the Rappahannock over which he is now retreating. We have again to thank Almighty God for a great victory. I regret to state that General Paxton was killed, General Jackson severely, and General Heath and A. P. Hill slightly, wounded.—R. E. Lee, Commanding."[33] —The weather is beautiful and it is hoped may enable us to profit by the victory. Longstreet's other two divisions are passing thro' and ought to be with Lee tomorrow, as the track at Ashland is said to be very little injured.

May 6th. There are few details of the general engagement which took place near Chancellorsville on Saturday, the 2nd. Jackson has lost his left arm and was shot through the right hand. There is a general sadness even over this multilation of the hero. He is, however, they say, doing well. The enemy appears to have recrossed the Rappahannock defeated, but not routed, and may again advance. We have not the genius to achieve decisive victories, it appears; and it is probably a problem not often solved, except with the concurrence of fortunate incidents, that a large army is defeated and routed by a very inferior one. The news from Alabama and Georgia is that sixteen hundred cavalry, or mounted infantry, were captured on the 1st, near Rome, Georgia. This is the force which made the "raid" into Mississippi at Meridian. From the Mississippi we hear that Bowen has fallen back from Grand Gulf, before overpowering forces.[34]

May 8th. The news comes in slowly from the late battlefields. The loss is heavy on both sides—that of the Yankees, perhaps, unprecedented in this war. Our own is placed at eight or ten thousand. The enemy has recrossed the Rappahannock without farther serious loss. It is deplorable that all our sacrifices of life and all our successes lead to no decisive result. Is this owing to our inferior numbers, or to want of solidity in the commands, or, finally, to want of genius in our commanders?—The weather turned quite cold yesterday morning, and fires are again very comfortable. The cavalry of the enemy are reported by General Lee to have probably re-crossed the Rappahannock.

May 9th. The worst news received yesterday was the death of Van Dorn at Spring Hill, Tenn., on the 7th. He appears to have been killed in a rencontre.[35] This and the wounding of Jackson are serious losses. The wounded are arriving and being sent off to other points.—Mamma went to the hospital last evening and stayed some hours assisting the poor fellows. It is a pity she cannot spare more time from her household duties to spend in these cares, as she is a very apt nurse.—The day is beautiful tho' the air is chilly. The Yankees appear to have formed the design of sending cavalry into our agricultural districts to destroy crops, implements, etc. It is stated that Kirby Smith has reached Alexandria with re-inforcements, and that he will be able to drive the Yankees back to Berwick.

May 10th, Sunday. The morning is balmy and beautiful. We have yet no news of the effect of Hooker's defeat on the Yankees. It is said that Lincoln has ordered another draft of 500,000 men. No doubt that the war will go on until at least the close of his administration. How many more lives must be sacrificed to the vindictiveness of a few unprincipled men! for there is no doubt that with the division of sentiment existing at the North the administration could shape its policy either for peace or for war. Yesterday some three or four thousand prisoners came down. It is tho't we have captured about 6,000 and lost 1,000, with eleven pieces of artillery and lost eight, and have gained ten or twelve thousand small arms. There are, besides some 1,500 to 2,000 wounded captured. On the whole the victory grows in magnitude each day—a peculiarity of Lee's victories.—There is no farther news from Vicksburgh or the Mississippi. In Tennessee there seems to be no immediate inclination for active operations.

May 13th. On Sunday evening we heard of the death of our great warrior, Jackson. He died about three o'clock of that day, of pneumonia, aggravated by causing himself to be bathed about the chest with cold water. Yesterday the body was carried in procession from the Governor's house to the Capitol, and lay in state during the day.[36] Today it is taken to Lexington where it is to be buried. I took Willie and Jessie to look at his face. The crowd nearly crushed us. Mamma had to be satisfied with a peep at the door where the coffin lay, in the room and over the House of Representatives below the Library.—There is no news of interest from the Mississippi, now the point most critical to us. It is believed, however, that Smith has beaten the enemy and driven him back to Opelousas. It requires some energetic genius to restore affairs in that quarter.

May 14th. It was said yesterday that the enemy was landing in force at West Point; in what force was not known. There is, of course, a demonstration on Lee's communications. Our losses at the great battles of the Wilderness are, perhaps, heavier than we anticipated. We have lost, no doubt, over two thousand prisoners, and ten pieces of artillery, while our killed and wounded will, I fear, exceed ten thousand. On the other hand we have captured eleven pieces and, perhaps, six thousand prisoners, killing and wounding fifteen thousand, thus making a total of twenty-one thousand, against our twelve or thirteen thousand. Had we not lost Jackson all would be well, but that loss would more than counterbalance a victory ten times as decisive.

Sunday, May 17th. The enemy has penetrated from Grand Gulf to Jackson, Miss., and our troops in that vicinity are said to have fallen back to Canton, on the railroad north of Jackson. The enemy's force is estimated at thirty thousand, but I cannot persuade myself that they would venture so far from their base with so large a force. It would be difficult to subsist them. I dare say ten or twelve thousand would cover their numbers. I trust General Johnston will yet send them back staggering, and that Vicksburgh will be maintained. The news is here today, that Vallandigham, for his bold speech against the Government of Lincoln, has been banished to the dry Tortugas.[37]

May 20th. On the 15th Grant attacked Pemberton near Edwards Depot, and, after a severe fight, our troops fell back beyond the Big Black. Johnston has eleven thousand men, and if he can but unite with Pemberton, all will go well. But affairs there are in a very critical condition. As

Vicksburgh has provisions for two months, I trust no disaster need be feared. The enemy has evacuated Jackson after destroying a good deal of property, and communication with Jackson is restored.

May 21st. Grant appears to have out-generaled us, and is now said to have invested Vicksburgh. If Johnston can bring about a junction of our forces, he will be able to fall on Grant with 25,000 men, which, with the garrison, of Vicksburgh, ought to be able to give him a disastrous defeat and restore our command of the Mississippi. As Vicksburgh has at least two months provisions there is good reason for hope that this effort of Grant's may prove his ruin.—Mamma amuses us often with accounts of the queer things that happen to her at the hospital, whither she goes every day, at the corner of Seventh and Cary Street. One man asked her to smoke his pipe until he could get ready for it, the pipe being filled and the bit paper in the attendant's hands.—Willie really distressed me today by striking Mamie on the nose so as to make it bleed because she had his marbles and some were lost.—We spent a half hour at the President's last evening. He is recovering but looks feeble still; has had fever and a cough.

May 23rd. Saturday. Pemberton was, I fear, badly beaten near the Big Black, and lost a good deal of artillery. He was, of course, greatly outnumbered. It is probable that Grant has fully forty thousand. Vicksburgh is reported to be closely invested. I fear it has not munitions enough for a long fight. It has not been possible to give them over perhaps 150 rounds per man. However, they have the means of making cartridges for themselves.—I spent the evening yesterday at the hospitable table of Mr. Haxall on Main Street. He gave us the largest variety of excellent wines I have ever seen. General Ewell was there with some dozen gentlemen.—Troops have been moving southward, since yesterday morning, doubtless for the west.

May 25th. The news is today that the enemy has been repulsed at Vicksburgh. I trust it may prove true. Should we be driven from the Mississippi it would have an important influence on the duration of the war. There is a painful rumor today that the outer lines of Vicksburgh have been forced and fifty cannon captured. It comes from the Yankees and is not believed. General Johnston telegraphs for large quantity of field ammunition and for percussion caps. There is great anxiety about affairs there. The people of Richmond are laughed at for their continually gloomy countenances. Officers from the field say they see more long visages here than anywhere else. It must be recollected that every blow struck at any point vibrates here; and we listen to and feel here every rumor of ill luck or of distress occurring in any part of the country.

May 26th. No later news from Vicksburgh. Hopes and fears alternate, but hope predominates. It cannot be that this strong city will fall an easy prey to a land attack. If it had a few thousand more defenders I should feel more easy.—The weather since Sunday has turned quite cool, and it is chilly enough for fires.

May 28th. A dispatch from a citizen at Vicksburgh, published this morning, assures us that "all is well" and that "V. holds out bravely." The Yankee papers publish it captured, but I trust they are too fast for the truth, and that it never will catch up with them.—Vallandigham, the Yankee opponent of his administration, is sent to the South, and has been left in front of Bragg's line. This is, of course, done to discredit his influence at home. The device is too shallow. He will, I suppose, be permitted to pass thro' and go to England or Canada. All "registered" enemies have been sent out of New Orleans, with nothing save what they could carry, and ten days' provisions. All who had relatives in the Confederate Army seem also to have been sent. It is reported that the number which have reached Pascagoula is four to five thousand.

May 30th. The public anxiety was relieved yesterday by a dispatch from General Johnston to the effect that Vicksburgh held its own manfully, and that a large number of the enemy had been killed and wounded. So great was the stench from unburied dead Yankees that Pemberton was burning tar barrels for disinfectants.

June 1st. No satisfactory news yet from Vicksburgh. It is to be hoped that Johnston will soon move upon Grant. The public will never forgive Johnston if he allows the city to fall without an effort to relieve it. He has probably thirty thousand men now.—The weather is very fine, but unless we can have rain soon our crops will suffer sadly, and without good crops what will become of us? It is indeed a sad and critical time to the Confederacy.

June 3rd. A dispatch to the Associated Press states that Grant summoned Pemberton to surrender and gave him three days. Pemberton replied that he did not require three minutes, that he would fight to the last, whereupon Grant attacked and lost very heavily. It is difficult to get reliable news. We know only generally that Pemberton was beaten on Baker's Creek, on Saturday, the 16th, that he lost largely in artillery; that a part of his force was cut off from him; that he retreated and abandoned his works on the Yazoo; that he was attacked in his lines repeatedly, and has signally repulsed every attack; and that in the battle of Saturday a portion of our troops behaved very badly, said to be Georgians.[38] All the available force of the enemy appears to be concentrated on this one effort and there is no disposition to attack at any other point. Lee will probably not let them alone, however, on the Rappahannock. — Mr. Ward,[39] late Commissioner to China, spent the evening here. Mamma was at Mrs. Jones where I joined her afterwards. A little party to Mrs. Stansbury, who leaves soon with her husband for Bermuda.—A refreshing rain last evening promises well for the crops, an absorbing topic just now.

June 8th. Nothing satisfactory yet from Vicksburgh. All we know that it is still holding out without any indications of weakness. At Port Hudson the enemy is said to have suffered a severe repulse—probably a newspaper report only. Nothing of Johnston's movements. If he allows Vicksburgh to fall his reputation will be gone past all redemption. Lee has moved his headquarters to Culpepper, and there has been some fighting below Fredericksburgh where the enemy crossed on a pontoon bridge in some force, for what purpose is not known.—Mrs. Stansbury, and her husband and Col. Wyatt Aiken, are staying with us. Last night we had a room full to tea; Mrs. and Miss Marye, Mrs. Jones and Dr. Habasham. I regret much to see Col. Aiken go back to his regiment. His escape at Antietam was so narrow that I fear he may fall in his next engagement. He was struck by six balls; two indented his scabbard, one struck and bent the tip of his drawn sword, one cut the sword knot, one cut his coat on the shoulder and the last went thro' his body, striking inside of the left nipple and coming out behind near the shoulder blade. His recovery was very extraordinary.—The weather is very cool and dry.

June 11th. On the 9th, a severe engagement took place on the upper Rappahannock, about Kelly's Ford, the enemy crossing in large force. The particulars are not yet received. Col. Sol. Williams, of North Carolina, was killed, also Major Farley of General Stuart's staff. General Rooney Lee, son of the General, was wounded. Two army corps were on this side, according to prisoners taken. Whether this attack was made to cover movements in another direction remains to be seen. Nothing definite from Vicksburgh, which seems in no hurry to be taken. The enemy are said to be ordering troops to the Gulf, and perhaps Mobile may have its turn. General Cooper[40] told me troops had been ordered from Charleston in that direction, and if not needed these were to join General Johnston, under Beauregard.—General G. W. Smith, wife and Colonel McLean, dined with us on a piece of lamb which cost $13.00!

June 13th. The city was disturbed yesterday by rumors of the approach of the enemy, who were said to have crossed the Chickahominy, and to have appeared in gunboats at the mouth of that stream. Our local troops were gotten in readiness, as there are only about five thousand men on the lines. We have organized our workmen into companies and armed them, making eight companies, altogether about eight hundred men.—No news from Vicksburgh, nor from Johnston. It is said that Kirby Smith has appeared near Port Hudson, but nothing is definitely known of his movements.

June 16th. A portion of Lee's army is moving thro' the Valley, and Winchester is again in our possession. What the movement means it is difficult to define. I trust we are not to have the Maryland campaign over again.—Vallandigham is now at Wilmingham and leaves for Bermuda by one of our vessels, the "Merrimac." He goes probably to Halifax.—No satisfactory news from Johnston or from Vicksburgh.

(It is somewhat singular that I should have omitted to notice the fall of New Orleans in its proper place, in recalling the events of the war. It fell on the 25th of April with little resistance, Forts Jackson and St. Phillip having been reduced after a gallant defence. It is impossible to contemplate this event even at this distance of time with any composure. Major General Mansfield Lovell was the commanding general, and is here now, attending the close of a court of inquiry into the matter. A dozen courts of inquiry could not reinstate him in popular estimation, or my own. He was unfit for his position.)

June 18th. General Lee chronicles another victory in his modest way. On Saturday and Sunday, Ewell, commanding 1st corps,[41] attacked the enemy at Winchester, and on the afternoon of Sunday compelled them to surrender, to the number of six or seven thousand,—so says the telegram of the press—with wagons, horses, fifty pieces of ordnance, etc., etc. Two thousand more were captured by General Johnson, at Berryville, being re-inforcements, so says the press, to Winchester. This clears out the Valley. It is greatly regretted that the miscreant Milroy escaped. He has been outlawed by proclamation, and would probably be executed if taken.—This good news will be tempered this morning by the news of the capture of the ironclad "Atlanta" at Savannah. She went out to fight two of the enemy's ironclads and was overpowered, it seems. The particulars are not yet known. She came from Europe as the "Fingal" with a cargo of general stores, and was purchased by the Navy, and covered with iron.—Colonel and Mrs. Stansbury left this morning for Bermuda, where he will be stationed in charge of a Depot of Ordnance Stores.

June 24th. The captures at Winchester reduced themselves as usual to about one-half the reported number, viz: to 29 pieces of artillery and 3600 men. Milroy escaped with the remainder. The news from Vicksburgh yesterday is that a second general assault was made on Saturday, and was repulsed with heavy loss on the part of the enemy, and that Kirby Smith had taken Milliken's Bend, which would cut off Grant's supplies.

June 28th. The Capital is again threatened by the enemy, but there is little alarm felt. All the able-bodied men are, however, embodied and armed, and thousands of hardy workmen are parading the streets today (Sunday) to confirm their organization. It is reported that the enemy have landed at the White House in force, but it is doubtful whether the force is at all formidable.—Jones' force is ordered here from West Virginia, the enemy having disappeared from there.[42] With the additional force the offensive may, perhaps, be taken on the Peninsula and Keyes[43] drawn into Yorktown and kept there. A rumor says that Harrisburgh has been destroyed. If not true now I presume it soon will be. The supplies derived from beyond the

Potomac are already valuable, one principal item being a thousand fine beeves.

July 1. It is my forty-fifth birthday, and I have now served twenty-two years in the Army. We had good news yesterday, part of which is true and a part doubtful. A flag of truce boat arrived yesterday at City Point, with eight hundred of our people, to carry away a part of the four thousand Yankees now on the Island (Belle Isle).— Our Signal Officer sent word to the Secretary of War that the officers of the truce boat said both Harrisburgh and York were in our hand. The latest papers from the North received by the same boat do not confirm the statement, which is therefore doubtful. It is true, however, that General Dick Taylor has captured the enemy's works at Berwick, capturing one thousand men and ten guns. This, it is asserted, gives us command of the Mississippi above New Orleans, and interrupts Banks' supplies. Vicksburgh resists successfully as does Port Hudson, where Banks' second assault was repulsed with great loss. Every one is looking anxiously to see what Johnston will do.— (On looking back over these disconnected entries I see that no mention is made of the capture of Messrs. Mason and Slidell, our ministers to England and France. They were taken from the British Mail Steamer "Trent" by Com. Wilkes, on her passage from Havana to Liverpool, and carried to Old Point Comfort. Hence they were conveyed to Fort Warren. They were liberated on the demand of England, and sent in a national vessel on board the English steamer, which conveyed them to England. The Yankee Government disavowed the act, but Wilkes again received a command. The affair caused great commotion in England, and was highly applauded in the United States. The Secretary of the Navy, Welles, even approved it officially. Ovations were given to Wilkes. After all this, when it was seen that England was preparing for war, Seward deliberately recanted, and declared the seizure unwarranted!)

July 2nd. It was said yesterday that Hooker was displaced, and General Meade placed in command of the Yankee army.—The President is ill today, and his physician is seriously alarmed about him. The death of the President would indeed be the most serious calamity that could befall us.—The Yankees are said to be approaching from the White House, and their pickets are in force at Tunstall's, about sixteen miles from here.

July 4th. I rode out yesterday and the day before to look after the fortifications, the President having expressed some anxiety on the subject of their condition of preparation. The inner line is one of detached works of considerable strength. The works are well constructed and in good order, commanding all the principal avenues of approach to the city. The second line, which is three-quarters to one mile farther from the city, is a continuous line of rifle pits, or covers, with places for field batteries. It is placed on high ground generally, but seems to me too much developed. I prefer the inner line, for the number of men we have. Our volunteer companies and militia are all in the field now, occupying the roads, while the regular troops take the field. Our troops skirmished with the enemy day before yesterday between the Chickahominy and the Pamunkey— one man killed and two wounded on our side. The enemy retired and was followed by our skirmishers to within a mile of the White House, so an officer who went out, informed me.

July 5th. The world [whole?] of the Confederate States will be somewhat astounded to learn today that Mr. Stephens has started for Washington, on what errand is not yet divulged, nor whether he will get there.[44]—The news yesterday was that Taylor and Magruder were on this side of the Mississippi, at Kenna, ten miles out of New Orleans, and that an attempt would be made to surprise Fort Jackson, which, it is said, is held by a small force of

negro troops. Ewell's troops were three miles from Harrisburgh on the 29th. Our news from Lee necessarily comes
thro' Yankeeland, now. Meade has succeeded Hooker in the
command of the Army. He was Captain of Topographical
Engineering when the war broke out.

July 9th. On Wednesday, Thursday and Friday, the 1st,
2nd, and 3rd, heavy fighting was going on at Gettysburg,
in Pennsylvania. General Lee had apparently concentrated
there all his forces; and Meade had done the same. We have
telegrams from Martinsburg that Lee has beaten Meade
and captured half his army. While the news, by the flag
of truce boat, was to the effect that Lee was retreating on
Sunday. Great uneasiness and anxiety is of course felt. It
is known that on Wednesday and Thursday, up to Friday
morning, our troops had held their positions. That was the
last news and came by way of the Yankee papers. Not a
word of any sort from Lee. The people on the flag of truce
boat last arrived, refused to give us papers, which was
suspicious of bad news to them. On the 7th we were told
by a telegram from Johnston that an officer had arrived
from Vicksburgh with the news that the place capitulated
on the 4th of July, the garrison being paroled and the officers retaining their side arms. The announcement is so
unexpected, after the assurances given heretofore, that it
appears incredible. There has been no confirmation of it
since. There is news that Taylor and Gardner[45] have driven
the remnant of Banks' force away from Port Hudson and
raised the siege of that place.—Mr. Stephens has returned
having done nothing with his mission, which, it is tho't
related to the rules which are to govern this war.—Maria
with her family is expected this morning. She will probably
stay here.—Some very daring things have been done on
the water on our side. A party of a dozen to twenty men
left Mobile, crossed the country to the Mississippi below
New Orleans, boarded a steamer lying there, secured the
crew, passed out thro' the blockading vessels and ran the
blockade into Mobile harbor safely, capturing and burning

COLONEL JAMES H. BURTON
Superintendent of Confederate Armories
Courtesy Miss Burton, Winchester, Virginia

a prize on the way; this was the "Fox." Another vessel
was cut out in the same way by a second party.—A few
days ago the city of Portland was startled by the disap-
pearance of the revenue cutter "Caleb Cushing" lying at
anchor in its waters. Lieut. Read,[46] of the privateer "Taco-
ny," after burning and destroying forty or fifty fishing
vessels, burned his own vessel, which was too well known,
and transferred himself and crew to another vessel, the
"Archer." He then boldly entered Portland harbor and cast
anchor. During the night he boarded the "Cushing," the
officers of which were absent, secured the crew and put to
sea. He was pursued shortly and overtaken by steamers
when he blew up his vessel, having transferred his crew
to the boats. He was captured and taken back to Portland.
Such things, together with the career of the "Alabama"
and "Florida," keep alive the spirit of the Navy, and prevent it falling into utter insignificance.

July 10th. The news that Vicksburgh has fallen is confirmed. It is indeed a terrible blow to our cause. It apparently sets us back indefinitely. It will enable the Yankees
to again recruit their armies, and will greatly depress our
credit abroad. It is believed that over twenty thousand men
were surrendered, and of these nearly seventeen thousand
have been fit for duty. Why an effort was not made to cut
thro' is not yet known.—General Lee has fallen back to
Hagerstown, where he has a secure position.—On the whole
our affairs look gloomier now than ever.

July 13th. Authentic news arrived from General Lee
himself on Saturday. The fighting on Wednesday, the 1st,
was destructive to the enemy; that of Thursday indecisive
and on Friday we were repulsed from the enemy's position.
Our loss is no doubt very heavy, but we appear to have
taken as high as ten thousand prisoners. General Garnett[47]
and Armistead[48] are killed, and a large number of general
officers wounded. The details are coming in slowly.—General D. H. Hill has been promoted to Lieut.-General (?)

and sent to the Mississippi.—We are again threatened by Yankee gunboats and transports in the James River.

July 16th. An Officer of Ordnance, writing from General Lee's headquarters, alludes to the operations of Friday as a "disaster" and as such I fear we must accept it. General Lee will make an attempt to retrieve it by some signal blow at the enemy.—Col. Aiken, 7th S.C., mentions his loss at 133, of whom 18 were left dead on the field. He states our total loss at about eighteen thousand; of this number five thousand may be prisoners. He thinks we have 11,000 prisoners. If this be correct the loss of the enemy in killed, wounded and missing cannot be less than 25,000—about one-fourth of his effective strength. Port Hudson has also fallen, and fears are being entertained for Charleston, which was attacked on Saturday and Friday last on its outworks on Morris Island. The enemy effected a landing on the south end of the island, where there was a small work, which our troops soon abandoned. The next advanced to the assault of Fort Wagner, on the north half of the island, but were decisively repulsed with a loss of 95 killed and about 250 wounded and prisoners. It is feared the enemy will succeed in taking Fort Wagner, and then reduce Fort Sumter from the north end of Morris Island.

July 17th. I saw the President yesterday. He is bitter against Johnston, as I judge from a single remark. When I said that Vicksburgh fell, apparently, from want of provisions, he remarked: "Yes, from want of provisions inside, and a general outside who wouldn't fight."—We have still no reliable accounts of the killed and wounded at Gettysburgh, or of the prisoners taken and lost there. It is certain that all of Pickett's brigadiers were killed, and his division wholly scattered. It could not be rallied until withdrawn far behind the field of battle.—The weather is disheartening, for three or four weeks it has rained constantly. All the crops in this part of the country will be lost—a sad loss to us. Can we believe in the justice of Providence, or must we conclude that we are after all wrong? Such visitations give me to great bitterness of heart, and repinings at His decrees. It is apparent that we are not yet sufficiently tried. The sins of the people of Charleston may cause that city to fall; it is full of rottenness, every one being engaged in speculations. When the fate of Lee's army was, as we tho't trembling in the balance at Gettysburgh, the interest was less vivid in it than in a steamer which was expected in; and when a gentleman communicated to a speculator that So-and-so, a well-known officer from Charleston, had been killed, he replied: "You don't say so; what's Calypro this morning," Calypro being a blockade stock! Her fall will be looked on by many as a righteous doom.

Editor's Notes

1 General William S. Rosecrans stubbornly repulsed the advance of Confederate forces under Van Dorn and Price on Corinth, Mississippi, October 3 and 4, 1862.

2 The Gorgas and Davis families always enjoyed a close friendship, which intensified after the war.

3 Van Dorn destroyed Grant's advanced supply base at Holly Springs, Mississippi, in a brilliant raid on December 20, 1862, and forced him to abandon temporarily his proposed attack on Vicksburg. *DAB*, XIX, 185.

4 Admiral David G. Farragut attacked Port Hudson, Louisiana, on March 13, 1863.

5 The Confederate States' Iron Clad *Palmetto State*, commanded by Flag Officer D. N. Ingraham, in company with the Confederate Iron Clad *Chicora*, Captain J. R. Tucker, attacked the Federal fleet blockading Charleston, South Carolina, on January 31, 1863, succeeded in causing the United States' Ships *Mercidita* and *Keystone State* to surrender and drove off the blockading squadron. A good account of this action is in Scharf, *History of the Confederate States Navy*, pp. 672-80.

6 Ambrose E. Burnside.

7 Joseph Hooker.

8 John Pelham (September 14, 1838-March 17, 1863) was affectionately known as the "boy major." He was one of the most able artillery tacticians in Lee's army and made his greatest contribution with

horse artillery. He was one of "Jeb" Stuart's favorites. Pelham was killed at Kelly's Ford, Virginia, March 17, 1863. *DAB*, XIV, 408.

9 Major J. W. Puller was killed in the above noted action near Kelly's Ford, Virginia, on March 17, 1863. See *War of the Rebellion: Official Records of the Union and Confederate Armies* (cited hereafter as *OR*), series I, vol. 25, part 1, 63; also Freeman, *Lee's Lieutenants*, II, 464.

10 A graphic account of the explosion of the Confederate Laboratory on Brown's Island on March 13, 1863, is to be found in the *Daily Richmond Examiner*, March 14, 1863. The accident incensed Gorgas, particularly since he had directed that the strictest safety measures be observed in the Laboratory. He instituted an inquiry into all the factors involved in the explosion. The report of the Board of Survey which made the investigation is appended to Chapter IV, volume 99 of the Confederate Records, War Records Office, National Archives, Washington, D. C.

11 Edward Sparrow.

12 General John McArthur.

13 Both of these firms did a large blockade running business.

14 President Davis proclaimed Friday, March 27, 1863, as a day of fasting for the Confederacy.

15 Ethelbert Barksdale.

16 General Francis A. Shoup, who was to participate in the defense of Vicksburg, Mississippi. See *B&L*, III, 489.

17 General Thomas C. Hindman had been in the Trans-Mississippi District. See *B&L*, III, 444-50 for the details of his various operations.

18 Isaac M. St. John was one of Gorgas's right-hand men. It was at Gorgas's suggestion that the separate Bureau of Nitre and Mining had been created and St. John made its chief. See Gorgas, "Ordnance of the Confederacy, I," in *Army Ordnance*, XVI, Jan.-Feb., 1936, p. 215.

19 For a full account of the riot see J. B. Jones, *A Rebel War Clerk's Diary* (reprint edition, 1935), I, 284-86; and for an account of the court proceedings following the demonstration, see the *Daily Richmond Examiner*, April 6, 1863.

20 This was probably the home of Mrs. Mary Jones.

21 John S. Mosby, the colorful partisan leader.

22 Bujac was one of the partners of the firm of Bujac and Bennett, arms manufacturers at New Orleans. J. M. Seixas was later appointed a War Department Agent at Wilmington, North Carolina.

23 For General John Pegram's report of his operations in Kentucky, see *OR*, ser. I, vol. 25, pt. 1, 171-74.

24 General Quincy A. Gillmore, U.S.A., commanding District of Central Kentucky. His report concerning Pegram's expedition is in *ibid.*, pp. 167-71.

25 This may have been Jeremy F. Gilmer, Confederate Chief of Engineers.

26 This was the highly important Erlanger Loan. For excellent discussions of this loan see J. C. Schwab, *The Confederate States of America, 1861-1865*, pp. 30-43; and Frank L. Owsley, *King Cotton Diplomacy*, pp. 400-06.

27 General Henry A. Wise.

28 George Wythe Randolph was appointed Confederate Secretary of War on March 22, 1862, and discharged the duties of the office with ability until his resignation on November 15, 1862. He served for a time, prior to his appointment to the War Department, as an artillery commander under Magruder on the Peninsula. *DAB*, XV, 358-59.

29 Senator George Davis. For his career in the Confederate Senate, see the *Journal of the Congress of the Confederate States of America*, vols. 1-6.

30 Captain R. M. Stribling.

31 Richard Taylor, only son of Zachary Taylor.

32 For an account of the citizen's response to the alarm, see the *Daily Richmond Examiner*, May 5, 1863.

33 The dispatch, in somewhat different form is in *OR*, ser. I, vol. 25, pt. 2, 768. It is dated May 3, 1863.
General Elisha Franklin Paxton was killed on the morning of May 3, 1863. Lee's final report of the Battle of Chancellorsville mentioned Paxton for "conspicuous courage in the assault on the enemy's works. . . ." See *ibid.*, pt. 1, 803; and Freeman, *Lee's Lieutenants*, II, 648 and n. Jackson received a wound which later, combined with pneumonia, proved fatal. Generals Harry Heth and A. P. Hill were not dangerously wounded. See *ibid.*, p. 570 and n; p. 649.

34 General John S. Bowen abandoned Grand Gulf, Mississippi, on May 3, 1863, and moved to Vicksburg. See *B&L*, III, 478.

35 This was true.

36 For detailed accounts of the reception of Jackson's body in Richmond, see the *Daily Richmond Examiner*, May 12 and 13, 1863.

37 Clement Laird Vallandigham, northern politician, was arrested on May 5, 1863, in Dayton, Ohio, and tried by a military commission for expressing treasonable sympathy with the enemy. Lincoln banished him to the Confederacy, from which he made his way to Canada. *DAB*, XIX, 144.

38 For a good account of the Battle of Baker's Creek or Champion's Hill, see J. C. Pemberton, *Pemberton, Defender of Vicksburg*, pp. 144-65.

39 This was probably John Elliott Ward, appointed envoy extraordinary to China by President Buchanan in 1858. Ward was a native of Georgia. See *DAB*, XIX, 426-27.

40 General Samuel Cooper, Adjutant and Inspector General of the Confederate Army.

41 General Richard S. Ewell was commanding the second, not the first, corps of the Army of Northern Virginia. He and General A. P. Hill had been appointed corps commanders during the reorganization of the army necessitated by the death of Jackson. See Freeman, *R. E. Lee*, III, 8-17, for details of the reorganization.

42 This force was the command of General Samuel Jones. He assumed command of the Department of Western Virginia about December 1, 1862, and was relieved on February 11, 1864. See Freeman, *Lee's Lieutenants*, III, 323-24.

43 General Erasmus D. Keyes, U.S.A., had some 10,000 men on the Peninsula. See *B&L*, III, 265.

44 Alexander Hamilton Stephens, Confederate Vice-President, went on a mission to Newport News, Virginia, ostensibly to discuss "several points of disagreement on the existing cartel for the exchange of prisoners." He was not successful in getting his proposition accepted by the Federals. For complete details see R. M. Johnston and W. H. Browne, *Life of Alexander H. Stephens*, pp. 444-45.

45 General Frank Gardner was the Confederate commander of Port Hudson, Louisiana. He withstood a siege of 43 days—May 26 to July 8, 1863—before he surrendered. He had about seven thousand men in his garrison while the besieging forces numbered some twenty thousand men of all arms. Toward the end of the siege, Gardner had only three thousand effective troops, and even these were starving. See *B&L*, III, 593-97 for a full account of the siege.

46 Charles W. Read, former commander of the C.S.S. *McRae*, took command of the "Clarence-Tacony-Archer expedition" on May 6, 1863, and was captured off Portland, Maine, on June 27, 1863. After serving as commander of the torpedo boats of James River Squadron, he was made commander of the Confederate ram *W. H. Webb*, and was captured when this vessel was destroyed near New Orleans on April 24, 1865. See *Register of Officers of the Confederate States Navy, 1861-1865*, p. 161.

47 General Richard B. Garnett.

48 General Lewis A. Armistead.

3 ★ ★ ★

Richmond Feels The Winter

July 28th, 1863. Events have succeeded one another
with disastrous rapidity. One brief month ago we were
apparently at the point of success. Lee was in Pennsylvania,
threatening Harrisburgh, and even Philadelphia. Vicksburgh seemed to laugh all Grant's efforts to scorn, & the
Northern papers had reports of his raising the siege. Port
Hudson had beaten off Bank's forces, and "the question"
said a Northern correspondent was only now, could he save
the remnant of his army. Taylor had driven the enemy
from the greater part of Louisiana, and had captured immense stores at Brashear. Winchester with twenty-eight
pieces of artillery and four thousand prisoners had fallen
into our hands. All looked bright. Now the picture is just
as sombre as it was bright then. Lee failed at Gettysburgh,
and has recrossed the Potomac and resumed the position of
two months ago, covering Richmond. Alas! he has lost fifteen thousand men and twenty-five thousand stands of
arms. Vicksburgh and Port Hudson capitulated, surrender-
ing thirty-five thousand men and forty-five thousand arms.
It seems incredible that human power could effect such a
change in so brief a space. Yesterday we rode on the pin-
nacle of success—today absolute ruin seems to be our portion. The Confederacy totters to its destruction.

July 29th. News rec'd today of the death of William L.
Yancey[1] at Montgomery. He was prominent in the earliest
days of the Secession movement, and went abroad as one

of the Commissioners of the Confederacy accredited to foreign governments. After his return he appears not to have
agreed with President Davis and has had little influence
even in the Senate.—It has rained not less than fifty days,
almost consecutively, probably forty-five days out of fifty.
The wheat which had been cut has sprouted in the shock.
The loss of the crop will be a most serious embarrassment
in feeding the army, especially if, as is threatened, the corn
crop should also be injured. The loss of arms in the Gettysburg fights will not fall short of twenty-five thousand, I
fear this with the losses on the Mississippi will carry the
losses up to seventy thousand, a serious matter to my department, but not, I hope, irreparable.—The singling out of
two Yankee officers by lot, to be executed by Burnside for
recruiting in Kentucky, is denounced by the enemy and they
have placed General Rooney Lee and Captain Windes in
confinement, and declare they will execute them. As
Buckner is said to have captured two Yankees recruiting
in Tennessee, I hope the true solution of the difficulty will
be found in the execution of these, and the liberation of
Sawyer and —————.[2] Since the fall of Vicksburgh, which
gives a large surplus of prisoners to them, the enemy exhib-
its a malignant spirit on the subject of exchanges.

August 1. No news yesterday of especial importance.
It appears to be admitted that Grant has gone up the
river with his forces—to what end no one seems willing
to predict. The bombardment still goes on at Charleston
with few casualties on our side.—We went to see Mrs. Cross
last evening. Saw there her mother Mrs. Ritchie, widow of
Ritchie the editor of the "Enquirer" in the days when that
paper was a power.[3]

August 2nd. The only good news appears to come from
the southwest where General Taylor is said to have defeated
the enemy in a recent engagement, capturing a large number of prisoners. It is not fully credited. The plans of the

enemy will soon be developed and then we shall know where
to look for the next attack. Mobile and Chattanooga appear
to be the points most likely to attract the enemy. Our
freight steamers continue to run to Bermuda, from Wilmington. This is our chief source of supply for arms; and
we get our steel, tin, zinc and various other articles in this
way. We also import leather, tools, hardware, medicines,
saltpetre, lead, etc., etc., in large quantities. We own four
belonging to my Bureau, and there are others running in
which the War Department is largely interested. Thus far
none of our vessels have been captured, tho' we have now
made some fifty trips out and back.—The weather is now
extremely warm. Ria is quite ailing and thin.

August 3rd. There was news of a cavalry fight at
Brandy Station, in which we lost Colonels Baker and Jones
killed.[4] Our forces got the worst of it, I fear. Longstreet's
corps is at Fredericksburgh, and troops were sent yesterday morning from here to replace some taken from Hanover Junction, to reinforce him.—The weather is oppresive-
ly warm, and I trust our troops may not have to undergo
heavy marches at this season.—Went with Mamma to
General Elzey's[5] to see Mrs. E. The General is a brave man.
He is surrounded by four or five youngsters for aides, etc.,
who were better in the ranks.

August 6th. Lee seems to have fallen back behind the
Rappahannock, and has his headquarters probably at
Orange C. H.—Charleston appears to be doing very well.
As long as Battery Wagner is maintained there need be no
apprehension.—No field officers were killed in the fight at
Brandy Station.—Col. Baker (now General) lost a portion
of his arm.—Johnston has established himself at Enterprize, on the Mobile and Ohio Railroad, so as to be in position to cover Mobile.—For four days past the weather has
been excessively warm.—Bayne and myself go out to breakfast with Mr. Freeland "at 7:30 to 8:00 a.m."

August 10th. No event of special importance has occurred. There seems to be a strong disposition to leave the
Confederacy to go abroad. Senator Gwynn[6] and his daughter went in the last trip of the Lee. Mrs. Greeham went also
lately, and now Mrs. ex-President Tyler applies for a
passage on one of our boats. We are burdened with applica-
tions and I suppose the private steamers carry as many as
can get on. The state of feeling in Mississippi is said to be
very discouraging since the fall of Vicksburgh. The soldiers
will not fight again under Pemberton, in whom they have
lost all confidence, justly or unjustly.—Of the forty thousand men whom we had in service on the 1st of May in
Port Hudson and Vicksburgh we shall never again, I fear,
reassemble six thousand—a large army lost at one blow.
Truly Grant's operations were fruitful of results. All now
depends for the present on Charleston. If we maintain it
against the determined attack preparing against it all will
go well. If not, we shall be driven from the seaboard entirely
to a line of interior defences. Then will our constancy com-
mence to be tested. I have my fears that many who now
seem determined will then suddenly show themselves *weak-
kneed*, and will quail before the storm. But I believe the
determined men will still retain sway and keep the timid
down; and the spirit of the people is still with the war, and
will continue so.—A good deal of sensation was created
by the appointment of General Lawton[7] as Quartermaster
General. Col. A. C. Myers[4] has hitherto been the Quartermaster General and has fulfilled his duties very well. Lawton is a graduate of the class of '39, but left service almost
immediately after graduating. He is a man of but moderate
ability. The President seems determined to respect the
opinions of no one; and has, I fear, little appreciation of
services rendered, unless the party enjoys his good opinion.
He seems to be an indifferent judge of men, and is guided
more by prejudice than by sound, discriminating judgment.
I have been surprised to hear his condemnation of men and
measures—in the field and in the Cabinet—yet apparently
without any idea that it was for him to correct them. He

sneers continually at Mr. Mallory and his navy, and is at no pains to conceal his opinions before that secretary. Yet he never controls him in any respect; nor will he yield to the opinion of the country which has long since pointed to a change in that branch of the service.

August 13th. There is little activity prevailing, the hot weather having, no doubt, its influence. The enemy are probably continuing their work on Morris Island for the reduction of Fort Sumter.—Mamma and I propose going to-morrow to visit Mr. Holcombe at his place beyond Lynchburg. We may stay eight or ten days.

August 24th. We returned yesterday from our visit to Mr. Holcombe. It proved to be a very pleasant quiet one, tho' the going and returning in the present condition of roads and of travel was wearisome. The children, (Willie, Minnie, and Ria) enjoyed the country exceedingly.—Here there is little knowledge of the war except thro' the newspapers, and the scarcity of articles of luxury and of wearing apparel.—Fort Sumter is suffering severely from the fire of the enemy's heavy rifle guns, and will probably be abandoned tho' the city will not therefore be given up. Beauregard telegraphs that he will defend Wagner and Sumter to the last extremity. Were I in his place, I should endeavor to level off the ruins of Sumter, and immediately place guns on it behind sand bags. It would be a task of difficulty and danger, and to be done in a great measure at night.—All seems quiet with the army of Lee, and his army appears to be nearly in its original good condition. General Bragg is threatened, and an advance into East Tennessee is considered the next most likely move on the part of the enemy.—Recent arrivals from abroad have given us a fair supply of arms, and will enable us to equip all the men we can raise.

August 26th. Fort Sumter has been nearly destroyed by the 8-inch rifle guns of the enemy, at a distance of 2 5-8 miles. This is certainly an extraordinary result, and is startling evidence of the superiority of modern artillery.— Mamma, and sister Maria, went yesterday on a pleasure trip to Drury's Bluff. Returned quite pleased. Mrs. Dain of the party, with whom Maria is much pleased. . . . — General Lee's army increases at the rate of six hundred per day.

August 28th. The city is again thrown into commotion by the appearance of the enemy, this side of the Chickahominy, after driving away a small force of ours stationed at Bottom's Bridge, of whom some were killed. The local organizations are again called out very much to our detriment, as work people charged with the supply of the army. —General Floyd[10] died on Wednesday, the 26th, in his fiftyeighth year. He has played a very important part in this revolution.

September 3rd. It appears to be certain that our forces have evacuated Knoxville in order to concentrate with Bragg's army at some point and advance. We shall soon, therefore, hear stirring news from that quarter. The shelling at Charleston still goes on, with no marked effect. After an examination of the present condition of Fort Sumter, engineers have decided that the Fort can be held, and it is still held. The probability is that the monitors will make their final attempt to run by during the night.—We are throwing projectiles at the rate of about twenty-five tons per day, one thousand rounds. The large imported gun, 12 3-4 inches, is probably now in position. The ball or bolt weighs 670 pounds; the gun 22 tons; English.—General Lee is in town in daily consultation with the President.— Willie saw him for the first time on Sunday, and sat in his lap. Willie seemed disappointed; thinks the General does not look "heroic!" Last evening Maria and Mamma met him at Mrs. Randolph's.

September 6th. The enemy has not yet succeeded in breaking thro' the defences of Charleston, and the bombardment seems to go on slowly. The 600-pounder is said to be mounted at White Point, on the battery.—Knoxville is evacuated by our forces, and probably occupied by the enemy. This is done for concentration with a view to an advance. I hope all will go well, but hitherto our advances have been lamentable failures. I have no doubt from all the signs that Lee is also meditating an advance against Meade; if not into Maryland. His army is again in excellent condition.

September 8th. After an obstinate defence Battery Wagner and Morris Island has been evacuated. This of course involves Fort Sumter, which has but one gun left. This result was expected after the first error of permitting the enemy a footing on the southern extremity. The next step will probably be the reduction of Fort Moultrie, and then the harbor will be effectually closed.—Johnston and Pemberton lost the public confidence. They are both now without commands.—A corps of Lee's army is ordered to East Tennessee to join General Bragg. Knoxville and most of the road from there to the Virginia line is in possession of the enemy. The best news is the falling of gold, which has gone down from 1500 to 1000 in a few days.

September 13th. I observe that I have omitted all mention of the foray of General John H. Morgan into Indiana and Ohio. He started from the Cumberland, traversed Kentucky—crossed the Ohio at or near New Albany—went around Cincinnati, and struck the Ohio at Buffington, fighting his way thro' and doing a vast amount of damage. All this in June and July. He was captured with three-fourths of his command, which consisted at first of about two thousand men, on the banks of the Ohio, the rains having so swelled that usually fordable river that he could not cross. He was lodged in the Ohio Penitentiary, for safe keeping. It was a most unfortunate enterprize, but would not have been disastrous, save for the unprecedented rains. —The great events transpiring about Gettysburgh diverted

attention from the daring exploit.—On Tuesday night the
enemy attempted to take Fort Sumter by assault in thirty
barges, at night. They were beaten off with the loss of over
one hundred prisoners, and four or five barges. I am pained
to hear of the bursting, on trial, of one of the two 600-
pounder rifle Blakely guns just received from abroad. In
fact the bursting is a sort of national calamity so much
was expected of these guns. A triple banded rifle, of the
Brooke pattern, has also burst. It is more than difficult
to make any of them endure anything like smooth bores.—
Longstreet's Army Corps has been going thro' the city for
East Tennessee ever since the middle of the week; Hood
first, then McLaws.[11] Pickett's Division remains here it
seems; White, Wise, and Jenkins' brigades,[12] heretofore
here, go to Charleston.

September 17th. Bragg has shown his usual readiness
for retreating, and has *retreated* us out of the whole of
East Tennessee—Rosecrans being in possession of Chattanooga, and Burnside of Knoxville, without the pulling of a
trigger. Two thousand men and guns and ammunition have
also been given away at Cumberland Gap, where a drunken
Brigadier, named Frazer, commanded. A cavalry fight occurred at and beyond Culpepper on Sunday, and our troops
have fallen back to Orange.—A brilliant thing was done a
month ago by Lieutenant Wood,[13] of the Navy. He captured
two steamers on the Potomac, each with forty men, and
two guns, by boarding with a force of some sixty men.
Wood is a grandson of General Taylor.—No firing has
lately been done at Charleston. The enemy is busy establishing guns at Cummings Point, no doubt with a view to shelling Charleston, at the distance of four miles.

September 23rd. On Saturday and Sunday, the 19th and
20th, a bloody battle was fought on the Chickamauga in
Georgia, near Chattanooga. The enemy was defeated with
the loss of, it is said, over fifty pieces of artillery, and is
retreating on Chattanooga. Our job is damped by the loss

of General Hood, who died under the operation of amputating his leg. He left here only two weeks ago scarcely able to manage his wounded arm. His loss is a severe one, second only to that of Jackson. Besides Hood we have lost Deshler, Helm and a General Smith[14]—and heroes of lesser note—too many, too many. The defeat of Rosecrans will have a telling effect as they hung their highest hopes on him. One division of Longstreet's corps only appears to have been engaged. I hope this victory may lead to the recovery of East Tennessee.—A Professor McCulloch, just from Columbia College, New York, spent the evening with us. He told us details of the cruel treatment of our wounded prisoners at Gettysburgh. He is a Baltimorean and has just quitted his professorship, rather late, but let our people come, even at the eleventh hour.

September 26th. Hood is not dead but has had his leg amputated and his condition was critical. Bragg telegraphs that he has taken seven thousand prisoners, thirty-six pieces of artillery, fifteen thousand small arms and a great many standards. The battle of Chickamauga will, therefore, rank as a great victory in the history of this great war. As, however, we do not hear that Rosecrans has abandoned Chattanooga the fruits of so great a victory are not yet reaped; and people are still in a state of anxious suspense, fearing that all this bloodshed may have been in vain, and that Tennessee may after all not be recovered. No doubt Rosecrans is being reinforced, and unless dealt with soon may become too strong to dislodge. The enemy is also operating in Western Virginia at and near Bristol, where some buildings were burned. A fight took place at Zollicoffer, where the enemy was repulsed. These are attempts to destroy the railroad, and have no design of permanent occupying. General S. Jones commands there on our side. Exchanges of prisoners will probably now again be effected, after the captures just made. The Yankees have of late had largely the advantage, and have behaved accordingly, refusing exchanges and keeping our men con-

fined in large numbers at Fort Delaware and other places.
—Dined at Mr. Harrison's[15] on Sixth Street. Mr. Mallory,
Secretary of Navy, and Mr. Memminger, Secretary of
Treasury[16] present. A dinner party of fourteen and very
tedious.

September 28th. The weather continues quite cool—a
slight frost on Saturday morning. The town was quite ex-
cited last evening over news that our cavalry was in rear
of Rosecrans, and our troops in position to cut him off. I
suppose it is too good to be true. It is difficult to "cut off"
a superior force, and if we can manoeuvre to force him back
on Nashville, by threatening his supplies, I shall be satisfied. The country expects, however, much more, even the
redemption of Tennessee entire. God grant its hopes and
wishes may be achieved. Everything is ominously quiet at
Charleston. The poor city is, I suspect, doomed to a fearful
ordeal. Ten thousand shells may be thrown into it in October, and the destruction those will create may be imagined.
But the city will be considered "defended" as long as the
site of it is in our hands. The "iron-clads" from England
are soon expected.[17]

October 3rd. On the 8th of September the enemy was
defeated in an attempt to force Sabine Pass, Texas, and
lost two steamers, carrying about 12 guns, which were disabled by the fire from land and were captured by our
troops.—The situation at Chattanooga is becoming less and
less encouraging as Rosecrans strengthens himself. We have
possession of all the railroads leading to the city, but he
appears to supply himself by wagon trains from Steven-
son. Should he be heavily reinforced he may resume the offensive and compel Bragg to retreat.—No movements seem
to be contemplated in Virginia. The firing has been resumed
at Charleston. Our firing produces little effect, as appears
from teams moving along the island despite the fire.

October 7th. No prospect of dislodging Rosecrans at
Chattanooga, and the blood of five thousand poor fellows

has been shed in vain. The President left for there yesterday morning. It seems to be believed that Mr. Mason has
withdrawn from England. General Polk, Hindman, For-
est,[18] and one other, are said to be in arrest at Atlanta for
disobedience of orders at Chickamauga.—The weather is
clear and cool.

October 11th. The situation remains unchanged, so far
as we know, at Chattanooga. The President is now there,
probably with a view to assuaging the *griefs* that have
arisen between the General (Bragg) and some of his chief
officers. There is no doubt that very heavy re-inforcements
have gone to Rosecrans from all directions. It would not be
surprising if he had near one hundred thousand men and
would soon have 130,000. With this force he can advance,
and I fear will be in Atlanta before the winter sets in.
Probably we may be able to defeat him in a pitched battle
before he reaches there. Meade has fallen back from the
Rapidan, and Lee has followed him, but no results are expected. The probability is that more troops will be transferred to Georgia, and I hope Lee will assume command of
affairs there.—Charleston will soon cease to attract attention, as it is practically in the hands of the Yankees, like
Savannah. It is an inland town now, and has ceased to be
of importance. The only port now left to us is Wilmington.—The weather is beautiful fall weather, clear, dry and
cool.—There seems to be no doubt that Mr. Mason has
withdrawn from London.—No further news of the ironclads, which seem to be expected to reach here somehow. I
have no faith in Mr. Mallory's proceedings I confess, nor
has any one else, except his wife.

October 16th. Several important cavalry fights have
taken place between Stuart and the enemy's cavalry, and
we have made some captures. The enemy has retired beyond
the Rappahannock, burning the bridges there, and is probably concentrating about Washington.—There are rumors
this morning of a heavy fight in the direction of Centre-

ville, but there is no probability of a general engagement.
General Johnston appears to have had a brush with the
enemy's cavalry in northern Mississippi between Grenada
and Grand Junction, and retired before a superior force,
they burning Wyatt.[19] His dispatch is from Oxford. I suppose he was trying to reach the Memphis and Charleston
Railroad with a view to cut off reinforcements coming
to East Tennessee from that direction.—Captain West,
Staff of General Zach. Deas was here last evening.—The
failure of the plan of battle before Chattanooga appears
to rest with D. H. Hill, on the extreme right. He could not
be found to receive the necessary orders in time, and was
too late in playing his part, which was to attack the communications with Chattanooga, and draw the enemy down
the river. From all I can learn our forces were not equal
in strength to the task undertaken. I have little doubt that
Rosecrans outnumbered the combined forces of Bragg,
which did not exceed 45,000 men.—At Charleston the old
story of firing at the enemy's working parties. The big
Blakely was fired there a few days ago with fifty-five
pounds of powder, with entire success. The range was very
good.

October 19th. The enemy advanced thro' Bristol to
Abingdon threatening the salt works,[20] but the news today
is that they are now rapidly retreating; probably because
they have learned that we are advancing upon Knoxville
from Georgia.

October 22nd. There is no military news of especial interest. The winter is coming forward and closing around
us drearily enough. I look forward to mid-winter with
anxiety. There is not food enough to sustain the population
here, and altho' there is abundance in the country the
limited means of transportation and the unsettled state of
the markets prevents food from reaching here. I fear we
shall see trouble on this score, especially should we have a

cold winter.—We have lately lost three ships in which we were interested: "Phantom" (our own); "Douro," of which the cargo was ours; "Venus" belonging to the Collie and Crenshaw line, of which we (the War Dept.) own one-half, and the cargo was entirely on Government account, consisting of bacon and quartermaster's stores. The vessels attached by my Bureau have been very lucky, the "Phantom" being the first and only loss; her cargo was partly saved.

October 28th. The military situation presents no new phase of interest. General Lee has returned to this side of the Rappahannock. The enemy still holds on to Chattanooga, but will not, I confidently hope, be able to continue there without fighting a battle to recover his communications. It was currently believed that Gilmore had gone with the bulk of his forces from Morris Island, whither no one knew. Rosecrans has undoubtedly been relieved from the command at Chattanooga, and is succeeded by Thomas, while Grant is placed in general command of the armies operating in Tennessee, Kentucky and Mississippi. Rosecrans is charged it is said with cowardice on the battle field, and other derelictions; most probably he has quarreled with Halleck.—We spent the evening at Mrs. Jones.—Weather cool but very fine.—The seizure of our rams by the English government is the chief topic of interest. Poor Mallory is ever unfortunate in his department. It is to be hoped he will have better success with those building in France. No one seems to apprehend that the French government will interfere with their delivery.—A capture by our cavalry of seven hundred prisoners with some wagons and artillery was made near London some day last week. Wheeler's operations on the Chattanooga and Nashville R. R. resulted in the capture of some prisoners and the destruction of eight hundred wagons, two thousand mules and large depots of stores, with "ten miles" of the track. Roddy[21] too is stated to have blown up an important tunnel.

October 29th. The great fear of every patriot at this moment relates to our currency. The vast over-issue of paper money has raised prices to such a pitch as to make the expenses of the Government enormous. The estimate of the Quartermaster General alone requires 54 millions per month after January 1st. This exceeds the limit fixed by Congress for issues of paper money by four millions. The fear is that a swift national bankruptcy is coming upon us. The poor suffer from this enormous inflation of currency. Beef is $1.25 per pound; butter, $4.00; eggs, $3.00; clothing is unobtainable, calico being $8.00 and $10.00 per yard; coffee is $8.00; sugar, $3.00, and so on. Shoes cannot be had under $50.00 and $60.00 the pair, for very common ones. God only knows where all this will stop. When we consider the absolute wealth of the South it is amazing that our finances should have been allowed to run into this ruinous condition. We are now in a condition to carry on the war for an indefinite period. There is breadstuff enough, and, tho' the inadequacy of transportation makes prices high in some parts, there is abundance for all if the total be considered. And we have war material sufficient —men, guns, powder—the real pinch is the Treasury, and I fear we must pass thro' a national bankruptcy to get out of that. Perhaps it is better that this paper of six or seven hundred million should come to naught and so relieve posterity of a debt too heavy to be borne.—On Monday last we went to the funeral of Mrs. Harrison, daughter of neighbor Mr. Freeland. She died suddenly; was quite young; had just lost her husband, and the occasion was one to excite deep sympathy. The minister, Mr. Hoge, prayed and preached over one and a half hours, during all of which time I stood up.—Yesterday I heard of the death of Colonel Dimmock, Chief of Ordnance of Virginia, of paralysis, the night before. His death was very sudden. He was a graduate of West Point, and somewhat advanced. Has been useful in this war.[22]

November 8th. During the last three days of October there was some fighting near Chattanooga. The enemy crossed the Tennessee below C. and drove our forces back this side of Lookout Creek, leaving them in possession of Raccoon Mountain. There is little doubt that we shall have to fall back from before Chattanooga, and then for the present abandon all of Tennessee to the enemy. It is a bitter tho't, but there may be even worse in store for us.—The President has visited all the principal points this side of the Mississippi and has probably just arrived in the city (9th).—Flour has sold as high as $125.00, and people are in fear of absolute want, with plenty in the country. Fear of impressment keeps farmers from sending their produce to market.

November 11th. On Sunday (8th) we heard of a fight which occurred beyond the Rappahannock in which the greater part of two of our brigades were captured, (Hay's La., and Hoke's N.C.). They were on duty over the river from the main body of the army. It is very strange how little success has attended the movements of Lee's army since the death of Jackson. On Sunday we heard also of the capture of the "Cornubia," and on Monday learned that Dick had been captured with her.[23] This is a heavy blow, in all respects.—The weather is quite cold with heavy frosts.

November 16th. The situation still remains the same at Chattanooga. The enemy, having possession of Raccoon Mountain, have no difficulty in getting supplied by river and railroad from Bridgeport, thus the last fruit of our victory at Chickamauga has slipped from our grasp. The general sentiment is undoubtedly that Bragg should resign his command, none of his subordinates having any confidence in him. I do not think that justice is done to Bragg. I think what he has done is not entirely appreciated, tho' it must be confessed what he has lost is most apparent.

November 17th. Rumors yesterday made Meade cross the Rappahannock and that a fight was imminent. It seems to have been nothing but a cavalry dash, tho' the ambulance committee was sent for—a certain sign that a fight was expected by General Lee.—The conduct of the French at the mouth of the Rio Grande is surprising; they have captured and carried to Vera Cruz, ships laden with arms and stores for us, under pretence that they were going to Matamoras, a port blockaded by them, and were intended for the Mexicans.[24] The apprehension of scarcity this winter weighs heavily on the minds of men. Nothing but prompt action on the part of Congress to rectify the currency will save us from great distress.

November 21st. General W. E. Jones did a handsome thing in capturing a force of Yankees at Rogersville in East Tennessee; about eight hundred were taken with four pieces of artillery, one thousand horses, wagons, etc.—The telegraph yesterday reports officially that Wheeler is at Knoxville with his cavalry and the infantry close by.—The loss of the "Cornubia," "R. E. Lee" and the "Ella and Annie," all laden with Government stores, is a very heavy one. It is a great reflection on our commanders that they allow their vessels to fall unhurt into the hands of the enemy. With the "Cornubia" fell into the hands of the enemy dispatches which excite no little interest, and will attract some ridicule upon us, as exposing all our plans. People abroad will distrust a nation that conducts its affairs abroad with so little skill.

December 6th. On the 25th of November our Army at Chattanooga suffered the worst defeat we have had during the war. Our troops were drawn up along Missionary Ridge, with the right resting near the mouth of Chickamauga Creek; the right under Hardee the left under Breckinridge. The enemy attacked about ten a.m., and at four broke thro' our left center, routing the left wing, with the loss of forty odd pieces of artillery and about five thousand prisoners, including the wounded. The right stood firm and covered the retreat. The enemy pursued next day, and after following our troops to Resaca was repulsed with loss by our rear guard under Cleburne, after which the enemy returned to Chattanooga, burning the bridges behind them. Bragg has asked to be relieved and it is believed that Hardee is in command. No permanent commander has yet been assigned. Our loss in killed and wounded is not heavy. Reinforcements are being sent to that Army, and it will soon recover its strength, but its morale is, I fear, badly shaken, despite the victory it achieved at Chickamauga. Longstreet's Corps was absent at Knoxville, endeavoring to force Burnside to surrender. Had he been on the left, as at the battle of C., all would have been well, and the enemy would have suffered a bloody repulse along the whole line as they did on our right.

In Northern Virginia Meade crossed the Rapidan at the lower fords, turning Lee's right, and moved his troops behind Mine Run, where Lee confronted him with the stream between them. An artillery duel was begun on the 27th, with no result. Meade again withdrew without loss a few days after, and both armies are again at their old quarters, Lee at Orange C. H.

The best news of late is the escape of General Morgan from the Ohio Penitentiary, with six of his officers and his safe arrival in Canada. It diffuses general joy.[25]

The bombardment of Sumter still goes on with little result. A few shells are now and then thrown into the city, and a little damage done.—Mamma has been confined to her bed with a painful attack since the 26th, and is still in bed, but declares she will get up tomorrow, cost what it will.—Provisions are very high, tho' not especially scarce. Flour has sold as high as $125.00 per barrel; potatoes, $15 to $20 per bushel; eggs, $3.; butter, $5.; sugar, $4.50 to $6.00; coffee any price, $20 on; gold sells at 20 and 22. I have just received a pair of shoes from Baltimore which at the lowest figures of domestic exchange will cost me $87.50. Congress meets tomorrow, and the first thing to be done is to arrange for the reduction of the currency—how is not yet agreed.

Monday, December 7th. Mamma is gaining strength, but has not left her bed today, as she threatened to do yesterday.—Maria is keeping house, and sways her sceptre with the energy of her character. A ham has, with my judicious carving, served as a daily dish for exactly seven days, and there is even a respectable remnant for tomorrow. It was a delicious Westphalia, and worthy the care bestowed on it.

Longstreet is at Rutledge, east of Knoxville, and asks for instructions, whether to wait for reinforcements or fall back to Bristol. The defeat of Bragg was less disastrous than first represented by himself. The chief loss is after all in the self-confidence of the Army, which success alone can restore to it. With the reinforcements sent to it, it will soon be in condition to act again. It is singular to reflect that had Longstreet remained with Bragg the left of our army where he commanded would have repulsed the enemy, as did the right, and Missionary Ridge, instead of a shameful defeat would have been a bloody repetition of Fredericksburgh; if on the other hand the movement on Knoxville had been carried as begun a few days after the battle of Chickamauga Burnside would have been captured, and Rosecrans's Army forced out of Chattanooga. If, again, Longstreet had been with Lee, or even two of his divisions, Meade would have been "ground to powder" as one of General Lee's chief staff officers expresses it, before he could have recrossed the Rapidan, during the last days of November. For the late advance of Knoxville the President is perhaps responsible, as he was with the Army of General B. when the movement began. It was an unfortunate move then, as the result proved. As Longstreet's Chief of Artillery[26] said then, it was undertaken too late, and in inadequate forces. It was early in November, six weeks after the battle of Chickamauga, before Longstreet marched!

Mr. Soule[27] called yesterday. He speaks with singular

clearness and force, and is a most attractive conversation-
alist. He has no hopes of an early termination of the war.

Friday, December 18th. Bragg having been relieved
from the command of the Army of Tennessee, Hardee remains in charge. A new commander is to be selected. Bragg
has expressed his willingness to serve as Chief of Staff to
General Johnston, and that combination may be made.—
The news came night before last that the enemy's cavalry
had reached Salem on the East Tennessee Railroad and
burned the depot. No troops to check him there, and he
seems to be at liberty to roam anywhere.—All is quiet on
the Rapidan.—The affair of the capture of the "Chesapeake," a steamer running from New York to Portland
creates great sensation at the north. Numberless steamers
went in pursuit of the abducted one, but she is not likely
to be caught. The escape of Morgan from prison a month
ago gives great joy.—The weather is very rainy, and the
roads will now be impassable for troops.—Mamma is still
in her room,—a whole month's confinement.

Sunday, December 20th. I have just been looking back
over the earlier pages of this journal, and do not regret
having begun it however trivial the entries may appear. I
feel sure it will interest my children when I am gone, and
that is one chief object.—Heard a few days ago of the loss
of the ironclad (Monitor) "Weehawken" off Charleston,[28]
with all on board. It is impossible not to rejoice over the
misfortunes of such enemies as we are fighting, cruel and
ruthless as they show themselves to be. Has war ever been
carried on like this before among civilized people? Homes,
gardens, crops, mills, and all intended for the use and
sustenance of the non-combatant population, are relentlessly and systematically destroyed. They are going to starve
and maltreat the inhabitants into submission. Slow-sighted
people, and policy as misguided as it is wicked. They
exasperate but do not subdue.—Johnston doubtless has

taken command of Bragg's Army unless Bragg remains as
his Chief of Staff, I do not hope good from the change. That
Army should, with the reinforcements it has had, be stronger than before its defeat at Missionary Ridge. It ought to
be 35 to 40 thousand strong. Longstreet is at Rogersville
still, probably. He prefers to stay there to supply his army.
—No progress made by the enemy at Charleston, save burning a home or so in the city by shells thrown from Cummings Point. A fire and twenty odd casualties are reported
at Fort Sumter.—Congress has not yet achieved action on
the currency. Does it reflect that their time may be worth
1 1-2 millions a day to the country!—There are rumors that
Mr. Seddon[29] intends to resign. . . . —I took Willie, Jessie
and Minnie to church with me, and heard a good sermon,
not from Mr. Minnegerode, bless him!

December 28th. Salem on the East Tennessee Railroad
was visited by Averell with three or four thousand men.[30]
Unfortunately a large stock of meat, grain and leather had
been collected there and were destroyed. Averell has escaped
with the loss of only a few hundred men, but they lost
nearly all their trains and some horses. It is very discreditable to the vigilance of our commanders. Longstreet appears
inclined to winter in East Tennessee, near Morristown.—
The Chesapeake, which was so adroitly captured by pas-
sengers, between New York and Portland, has been recaptured at Sambro, N. S., by the "Ella and Annie," one
of our blockade runners just captured.—Johnston has
formally assumed command of Bragg's Army.—Mamma is
still confined to her room, but is gaining strength daily.—
Christmas was not a merry one to me, and I passed it very
quietly, almost sadly, at home.

January 5th, 1864. No military event of any sort has
happened lately; rain and consequent mud has closed all
operations. A few shells are thrown into Charleston occasionally, and on Christmas Eve and morning, the city
was heavily bombarded. One killed and one at least (a

woman) mortally wounded.—The New Year came in very cold, but it is now again raining. Mamma is up and about but has not yet come down.

January 10th. The arrival of General Jno. H. Morgan created quite a stir here on Friday. The city authorities and the Governor received him at the Ballard House, and gave him a handsome reception.—No military events have transpired. Charleston seems to be given up by the enemy who only throw an occasional shell. Having sealed the harbor against commerce they consider their task no doubt half accomplished. A land attack is probable toward Spring. Wilmington too, it is believed, will be attacked by land.— Lee's army numbers now less than thirty thousand infantry. With cavalry and artillery it may be placed at thirty-eight thousand men. Longstreet has perhaps 22,000, including a large cavalry force, say eight thousand. General S. Jones, in West Virginia, has, I suppose, six to eight thousand, and there are say ten thousand men here and at Petersburgh. This will constitute a force of about eighty thousand men in and upon the borders of Virginia, of whom sixty thousand could be concentrated in five or six days on any point. Is not this a force large enough to defeat any force the Yankees can probably bring against us?—General Early[31] is operating in the lower valley of the Shenandoah, to get beef, of which the army is in great need. We shall get through the winter without manifest suffering, tho' shoes and blankets are still wanting.—In the midst of these gigantic wars people will still amuse themselves, and I went with Maria and B. to see some charades at Mrs. Semm's. They were very good, and Mrs. Semm's especially successful, and hence, I suppose, the charades.

January 17th. Sunday. There is little news of a military character. In consequence of the assignment of Beast Butler[32] to the command at Fortress Monroe the exchange of prisoners appears farther off than ever. We have about 35,000 prisoners in their hands against say 16,000 in our

possession.—General W. E. Jones seems to be doing a little
work in East Tennessee, having lately captured 360 prisoners, with some wagons, three pieces of artillery, etc. It is
stated that with his brigade he has captured over 1200 men
in the last two months. General Maury[33] at Mobile, and
General Whiting[34] at Wilmington, both apprehend early attacks on their places respectively. Our Armies are filling
up, and will, I hope, be strong enough for their work by the
1st of May.—A law abolishing all *substitution* has just been
passed.[35] While I don't think this will materially strengthen
the army, it will give general satisfaction. A scheme of
restoring the currency passed the House yesterday; its
features are not known.—The Yankee Congress appears
disposed to prosecute the war with vigor, tho' the opposition amounts to nearly seventy votes, on a test question.—
General Morgan came to my office during the week. He is
a very handsome man, about six feet high, with light brown
hair and blue eyes, about 37 to 40 years old. His hair had
not quite recovered from the cropping it received in the
Ohio penitentiary. Captain Hines, one of his escaped com-
rades, was with him, a modest young-looking man of active
build.[36] These men will be heroes of history.—On Wednesday evening, at Mrs. Randolph's charades, there were present Hood, Stuart, Buckner, Elzey,[37] all Maj. Generals—
and several Brigadiers. Stuart is fond of society, but entirely abstemious as to drinks. Last night I met an officer,
Major French,[38] in the Commissary Department, who had
never tasted liquor. Would these were the rules in the
Army; unfortunately they are rare exceptions, the vice of
drinking being nearly everywhere prevalent. . . .

January 21st. Movements reported seem to indicate
designs against Mobile. Its present armament would have
been considered powerful three years ago, and with the land
force at Meridian under General (Bishop) Polk, it may be
considered pretty well prepared for defence. A couple of
good cargoes have lately arrived there for us from Havan-
na. Charleston has daily some 150 large shells thrown into

it from the distance of four miles, without very great effect, as reported.—Troops are today moving thro' the city southward, probably to be prepared to assist Wilmington. Longstreet seems to be active and some successes are reported in that quarter.—The Bill for improving the currency has passed the House, and is before the Senate. Its features are not known, but is doubtless sufficiently stringent. The danger now seems to be a too eager disposition to sacrifice everything to putting men in the field at the expense of the industrial interests.—A letter from Dick received by last flag of truce assures us he is well and well treated, but tired of his confinement and longing to be exchanged. The Commandant of Fort Warren is Colonel Dimick,[39] a good officer of the old service, and humane.

January 31st. Slight events of varied character have occurred in East Tennessee. General Vance, commanding in Western North Carolina with about fifty men has been captured, by the Yankee General Sturgis.[40] He was returning from a partially successful foray into the Yankee lines. —Under Longstreet General Martin[41] met with a reverse, losing two pieces of artillery and several hundred men, killed, wounded, and missing. The troops are getting supplies of food and clothing, and their spirit is represented as generally good. The ranks are decidedly filling up, as is evident from the number of arms called for. There is a disposition in the Senate, probably instigated by the Secretary of War, to drive the enginery of war under too great pressure. A Bill has passed it to place in the Military Service, for details, all men between 45 and 55. This is unnecessary. In such a war as this—a war for national existence—the whole mass of the nation must be engaged. It must be divided into those who go to the field and fight, and those who stay at home to support the fighting portion —supplying all the food, and material of war. Between the age of eighteen and forty-five has been fixed on for the fighting population—the rest must be devoted to agriculture, arts, mines, and manufactures. It is simply absurd to

call on all to fight. Some must labor or all will starve. There
is much crude legislation going on, but we shall work thro'
this revolution with some blunders.—General Pillow came
to my office yesterday. He and I served in Mexico together
—at least we were there together. He is charged he says
with organizing two brigades of cavalry to cover northern
Alabama. He is a man of energy and ability, and, were he
content to *serve*, would, I think, be very useful; but his
great ambition leads him to seek commands to which his
military status is hardly equal. To a General by whom he
would be controlled he would be very useful.

Editor's Notes

1 William Lowndes Yancey was a constant agitator for Southern
independence. In March, 1861, he was sent to England and France
as Confederate Commissioner. He returned in 1862 and was elected
to the Confederate Senate, where he served until his death at Montgomery, Alabama, July 27, 1863. See *DAB*, XX, 592-95.

2 On July 6, 1863 "The Federal captains in prison at Richmond, Va.,
draw [drew] lots for two to be shot—in retaliation for the shooting
of Capts. Corbin and McGraw as spies, at Johnson's Island, on May
15, by order of Gen. Burnside. Capts. John Flinn, 15th Indiana, and
H. W. Sawyer, 1st New Jersey Cavalry, selected." See Lewis Collins,
History of Kentucky, I, 125. The Captains Corbin and McGraw were
William F. Corbin and T. G. McGraw. See *ibid.*, p. 122.

3 Thomas Ritchie founded the Richmond *Enquirer* in 1804, and made
that newspaper a power in the country and the "Democratic Bible."
For a fine sketch of Ritchie, see *DAB*, XV, 628-29.

4 These were probably Lawrence S. Baker and William E. ("Grumble") Jones. Jones was a brigadier.

5 Arnold Elzey.

6 William M. Gwin, who served as United States Senator from Calif-
ornia from September 10, 1850, to March 3, 1855, and from February
16, 1857, to March 3, 1861. He was then connected with the Confederacy. See O. M. Enyart (comp.), *A Biographical Congressional
Directory, 1774 to 1903*, p. 568.

7 Alexander R. Lawton, lawyer, objected to his assignment as quartermaster-general as he had previously commanded an infantry brigade

in Lee's army. See in particular *B&L*, II, *passim;* and index to *B&L;* also *DAB*, XI, 61-2.

8 Abraham C. Myers had served as chief quartermaster of the Army of Mexico, under Winfield Scott, from April to June, 1848. Appointed first quartermaster-general of the Confederate Army, he worked under drastic handicaps, such as scarce funds and poor transportation. He did the best he could but was the target for much severe criticism and Davis supplanted him with Lawton. See *DAB*, XIII, 375-76.

9 Stephen R. Mallory, Secretary of the Confederate States Navy.

10 John B. Floyd, former governor of Virginia and Secretary of War under Buchanan. See *DAB*, VI, 482-83. Floyd and Gorgas were good friends, which at times, during Floyd's administration of the War Department, had been a real help to Gorgas.

11 Lafayette McLaws. He later was court-martialled, but was found not guilty and sent to command the District of Georgia in the Department of South Carolina, Georgia and Florida. See Freeman, *Lee's Lieutenants*, III, 298-303; 305-06; 310-11; 373; 435.

12 The agitation created by the rumored shuffling of the brigades stationed near Richmond culminated in the assignment of Micah Jenkins' brigade to Longstreet's Corps for operations with the Army of Tennessee; Pickett was left on the Richmond sector; G. T. ("Tige") Anderson's and Henry A. Wise's brigades went to South Carolina. See *OR*, ser. I, vol. 29, pt. 2, 713; also Freeman, *Lee's Lieutenants*, III, 224.

13 John Taylor Wood resigned as lieutenant in the United States Navy on April 12, 1861. He was made a Captain in the Provisional Confederate Navy on February 10, 1865. He captured the United States steamers *Satellite* and *Reliance* on August 23, 1863, and the schooners *Golden Rod*, *Coquette* and *Two Brothers* on August 24, 1863. He commanded the *Tennessee* in 1864 and served as Aide to the President, 1863-65. See *Register of Officers, Confederate Navy*, p. 216.

14 General Hood was not killed. General James Deshler was killed while leading his brigade at the Battle of Chickamauga, Georgia, September 20, 1863. General Benjamin H. Helm was killed the same day, leading his brigade in an assault on the enemy's entrenchments. The "General Smith" mentioned by Gorgas was probably General Preston Smith. He was killed on September 19 assaulting part of the enemy's log breastworks. See *B&L*, III, 656, 655, 652 for details of the death of these generals.

15 This may have been at the home of Burton N. Harrison, secretary to Jefferson Davis.

16 Christopher Gustavus Memminger served as Confederate Secretary of the Treasury from the founding of the Confederate Government until his resignation on June 15, 1864. See *DAB*, XII, 527-28; and H. D. Capers, *The Life and Times of C. G. Memminger*.

17 These were probably the "Laird Rams." These were two double-turreted, ironclad vessels—one equipped as a ram, which were ordered in 1862 from John Laird and Sons, shipbuilders, of Berkenhead, England. The North, fearful lest the English allow them to put to sea, brought pressure to bear and the British government formally seized them in October, 1863, and purchased them for the Royal Navy. See. J. T. Adams and A. V. Coleman, eds., *Dictionary of American History*, III, 228.

18 General Leonidas Polk was a bishop of the Episcopal Church. Serving as corps commander in the Army of Tennessee, he was relieved of command by Bragg after the Battle of Chickamauga for delaying an attack. Davis restored him to troops. He was killed at Pine Mountain, near Marietta, Georgia, on June 14, 1864. T. C. Hindman was relieved of his command, along with Polk, for failing to obey orders. Later, Bragg relented and restored Hindman to his command. Forrest had a violent quarrel with Bragg, accusing him of jealousy and discrimination, and refused to serve under him. For details of Bragg's controversy with his subordinates, see S. F. Horn, *The Army of Tennessee*, pp. 283, 290.

19 An official dispatch from General J. E. Johnston recounting the activities of the Union cavalry in pursuit of Confederate forces in Mississippi was published in the *Daily Richmond Examiner* on October 16, 1863. The message was received by Johnston from Oxford, Mississippi. He, in turn, relayed it from Meridian.

20 These were the important works at Saltville, Virginia. The Confederate States depended heavily on the salt output of these works for a supply of this much needed commodity. For a general study of the problems involved in obtaining salt in the Confederacy, see Ella Lonn, *Salt as a Factor in the Confederacy*.

21 General Phillip D. Roddey commanded a brigade in Forrest's cavalry corps. See *B&L*, IV, 759.

22 Colonel Charles Dimmock. Gorgas had had an unpleasant altercation with Dimmock in 1861 regarding the transfer of some of the gun machinery captured at Harper's Ferry, Virginia, to the Confederacy. Considering the severity of this quarrel, Gorgas's comment, in the text, is quite charitable. For the correspondence relating to the Harper's Ferry affair, see *OR*, ser. IV, vol. 1, 468-73.

23 Richard H. Gayle was commanding the blockade runner *Cornubia* when she was captured on November 8, 1863, at Wilmington, North Carolina. Imprisoned in Fort Warren, Boston Harbor, he was exchanged and later captured again. See *Register of Officers, Con-*

federate Navy, p. 68; also "The Capture of a Confederate Blockade Runner: Extracts from the Journal of a Confederate Naval Officer," in *The North Carolina Historical Review*, vol. XXI, no. 3, April, 1944, 136-38.

[24] This policy of the French had caused comment in October. John B. Jones, the Rebel War Clerk, thought the French had mistaken some Confederate supplies for some sent by the United States to the Juarez forces. See Jones, *A Rebel War Clerk's Diary* (reprint edition, 1935), II, 74.

[25] John Morgan escaped from the Ohio Penitentiary, with six of his officers, on November 26, 1863.

[26] General Edward Porter Alexander. He was the author of a book entitled *Military Memoirs of a Confederate*, published after the war.

[27] Pierre Soule, fire-eating American minister to Spain, 1853-54, had tendered his services to the Confederacy in September, 1863, and received an honorary brigadier-generalship—his further rise in Confederate affairs being blocked by the hostility of Jefferson Davis. See *DAB*, XVII, 405-07.

[28] The United States Monitor *Weehawken* foundered at her anchorage in Charleston Harbor on December 6, 1863, apparently from leakage and failure of her pumps. See *Official Records of the Union and Confederate Navies in the War of the Rebellion*, ser. I, vol. 15, 161-70.

[29] James A. Seddon was appointed Confederate Secretary of War in November, 1862, soon after the resignation of G. W. Randolph. See *DAB*, XVI, 545-46. He resigned in February, 1865.

[30] General William W. Averell, commanding Union cavalry in Tennessee. For the "Salem Raid" and other details of the career of this able man, see *DAB*, I, 441-42; C. D. Rhodes, *History of the Cavalry of the Army of the Potomac*.

[31] Jubal Anderson Early.

[32] General Benjamin F. Butler, whose administration of the captured city of New Orleans brought down the wrath of the world on the United States. For his many high-handed acts while commanding the city—in particular the issuance of his famous Order Number 28, or the "Woman Order"—he earned the sobriquet of "Beast." See *DAB*, III, 357-59; also, for his official correspondence and that of Confederate authorities regarding his activities, see *OR*.

[33] General Dabney H. Maury, nephew of Matthew Fontaine Maury, the famous oceanographer. Maury conducted an able defense of Mobile, though he lost the harbor defenses to Admiral Farragut in August, 1864. In 1865 Maury held off the combined force of Farra-

gut's fleet and General E. R. S. Canby's army of 45,000 men, with only 9,500 effectives from March 27 to April 12, whereupon he retreated to Meridian, Mississippi. See *DAB*, XII, 427-28.

34 General William H. C. Whiting had, in 1845, established the highest graduate standing ever attained at West Point. Put in command of the military district of Wilmington, North Carolina, he made the Cape Fear River a haven for Confederate blockade runners and made Fort Fisher, at the mouth of the river, the strongest bastion in the Confederacy. Captured while defending this fort on January 15, 1865, Whiting died, of wounds suffered during the defense, at Fort Columbus, Governor's Island, N. Y., on March 10, 1865. See *DAB*, XX, 136-37.

35 This was "An act to prevent the enlistment or enrollment of substitutes in the military service of the Confederate states." See *Statutes at Large of the Confederate States*, Statute IV, Chapter III. The Act was approved December 28, 1863.

36 Captains Thomas H. Hines, J. C. Bennett, L. D. Hockersmith, J. S. Magee, Ralph Sheldon and Samuel Taylor escaped with Morgan from the Ohio Penitentiary at Columbus, Ohio. See *B&L*, IV, 422-23; also C. F. Holland, *Morgan and His Raiders*, 268-87.

37 John B. Hood, J. E. B. Stuart, Simon B. Buckner and Arnold Elzey.

38 Major S. Bassett French was on duty with the Bureau of Subsistence in Richmond, under Commissary-General L. B. Northrop. See index to the *OR* for French's correspondence.

39 Colonel Justin Dimick was graduated from West Point on July 1, 1819, and assigned to the cavalry. He participated in the Seminole War and was brevetted for gallantry. He was also brevetted for meritorious conduct in the Mexican War. From October 26, 1861 to January 1, 1864, he commanded the Prisoner of War Depot at Fort Warren. See *Cullum*, I, 213-14.

40 General S. D. Sturgis commanded United States cavalry forces which captured General Robert B. Vance, brother of Governor Zebulon B. Vance of North Carolina, and 51 prisoners on January 14, 1864, at Cosby Creek, Tennessee, twenty-three miles from Sevierville. For Union accounts of this affair, see *OR*, ser. I, vol. 32, pt. 1, 73-5; for Confederate accounts, see *ibid.*, pp. 76-7.

41 For a report of General William T. Martin's reverse in a severe engagement with strengthened Union cavalry, and General Longstreet's request for cavalry reinforcements as a consequence, see *OR*, ser. I, vol. 32, pt. I, 149-50.

4 ★ ★ ★

General Lee Digs In

February 4th, [*1864*]. A party of 150 Yankees landing from a steamer at Smithfield on the Nansemond were nearly all captured and the steamer destroyed last week. The news came this morning that General Pickett had encountered the enemy eight miles from Newbern and had killed and wounded nearly one hundred and captured 200 and two pieces of artillery. One gunboat was also destroyed. The object of the expedition—the capture of Newbern—was not attained it seems. The movements of the enemy down the Mississippi, coupled with the evacuation of northern Mississippi, have led to the surmise that Mobile is to be attacked.—I saw an officer from Charleston today. The injury done to the city by the shelling is by no means great. —The country is still awaiting with eagerness the action of Congress on the currency. I fear it is too late to redeem it now. Since Congress met an additional hundred millions have no doubt been added. Their action to do good should have been prompt.

February 14th. During the week 109 of the Yankee officers escaped from the Libby prison, by making a tunnel under the street some sixty feet long. Thirty only appear to have been recaptured. It is a serious misfortune just as the exchange question is pending—diminishing our prisoners so sensibly.—Sherman is moving eastward from Vicksburgh, and when last heard of was reported at Shorter, half way from Jackson to Meridian.—A demonstration has also been made from Jacksonville toward the interior of Florida,—and at Charleston on the lines on John's Island. Both advances were repulsed. Some think Sherman's movement threatens Mobile, others that its only object is to devastate upper Mississippi and Alabama. The enemy's movements are now no doubt partly political. They try to get possession of the capitals of the States and institute State governments, for effect on the next elections. All such government would be subservient to Lincoln.

February 18th. Nothing definite concerning Sherman's movements. An attack appears to have been made at Grant's Pass, without success. General Polk has withdrawn his forces behind the Tombigbee. It is still doubtful whether Sherman's object is Mobile or to devastate the grain growing region about and above Demopolis—perhaps a march on Selma. Fifty-four of the Yankee officers have been recaptured. The prisoners on Belle Isle are being sent to Americus, Ga., at the rate of four hundred a day.—The currency and tax bills are at last out, and are sufficiently stringent to satisfy the most craving.[1] These, with the Military Bill,[2] will form a series of measures calculated to restore courage to the timid—and it is needed.—The weather is the coldest known here for many years, it is said.

Sunday, 21st. General Bragg spent Tuesday evening with us. Willie now boasts the personal acquaintance of two Generals (Lee and Bragg) three Lieut.-Generals (Hood, Ewell and Hill, A.P.). Bragg was talkative. We had a good game of whist,—Mr. Lyon, Capt. Brown[3] and myself— some good supper and egg-nogg; altogether a pleasant evening.—Sherman, as far as heard from, has not advanced east of Meridian, but is no doubt doing great damage to the Railroad and destroying the corn, of which there is great store in that region, and doubtless some cotton.—Mr. Holcombe was here this evening with Mrs. Jones. He goes to Halifax on a mission in relation to the "Chesapeake."[4] He is not very hopeful about the currency.

Thursday, March 3rd. The city has been in commotion since Monday from a threatened attack of cavalry, coming from the Army of Meade, and commanded by Kilpatrick. On Tuesday they appeared on the north side of the city and shelled the batteries, or outer defences. They were driven off with the loss on our side of one killed and five or six wounded. This on the Brooke turnpike. About the same time they appeared about five miles from the city on the plank road, and were met about sundown by the battalion from the Armory here, which lost three killed or mortally wounded, and four or five wounded more or less severely. The enemy were finally driven off they losing eight or ten killed and a good number wounded. Some fifty of our men were taken prisoners and paroled by the Yankees. Yesterday it was reported that the enemy were approaching Bottom's Bridge, but it is again said that they have retired. The local forces are, however, again sent out on the lines tonight.

Last week we had news of a considerable success over the Yankee forces invading Florida from Jacksonville. They marched westward ten thousand strong, it is said, to within ten miles of Lake City (Alligator) where they were met by our troops under General Finnegan, rated at four or five thousand, and defeated with the loss of several thousand killed, wounded and captured, and five pieces of artillery.[5] The tide of invasion seems therefore to have been thus far turned back in Mississippi and in Florida.—General Bragg is in command here, having been assigned to duty with the President, to direct under him "the military operations of the armies of the Confederacy."

March 4th. Today were captured Col. Dahlgren and his command of raiders—outlaws—bandits. He was dead, but on his body were found the orders to his command, which were to enter the city, set it on fire in as many places as possible, liberate the prisoners, capture and kill the President and his Cabinet, and to commit every possible horror on the Capital. What beasts and murderers. Hereafter

those that are taken will not be heard of.—We have passed
a social pleasant evening. Mrs. Robinson and Mrs. Jones,
Colonel DeLagnel[6] and Judge Robinson.—Heard of the arrival at Charleston of the "Don" (blockade runner) and of
two vessels at Wilmington, perhaps three: Steamer "City
of Petersburgh" and "Alice"—some from Nassau, and some
from Bermuda—with provisions, lead and general supplies.

March 6th. A flag of truce boat with 900 prisoners arrived yesterday. It is hoped this may lead to the resumption
of the cartel. We shall not, however, return a like number,
but probably a number in proportion to the whole number
held by each.—The sinking of the sloop of war "Housatonic," of thirteen guns, by the torpedo "David"—a submarine affair—is chronicled.[7] Unfortunately the "David"
was, it is feared, lost with all her crew.

March 11th. The affair at Okolona in which Forrest
with very inferior force repulsed Smith and Grierson[8]
seems to have been a very handsome one. Its result too was
the retreat of Sherman, whose plans were thus entirely
deranged.—Over three hundred of the late *raiders* have
been captured—pity that more of them were not killed.—
The shelling at Charleston still goes on slowly, without it
is said much additional effect. Three torpedo boats are
ready there to make an attack on the gunboats or ironclads. It is said the wonder boats now go to sea at night
to avoid being blown up.

March 13th. The failure of their military operations
seems to have had a decided effect on gold among the
Yankees. It has gone to 169. I trust a few more failures
will send it to 200.—Partial exchange of prisoners is going
on; 600 were delivered to us yesterday, I learn. We return
about two-thirds.—Willie and I took a walk of seven miles
today, the weather being very pleasant.

March 16th. Numerous torpedo boats are building, to
the number of say thirty, with the view of destroying the

blockading vessels at Charleston. These are cigar-shaped, have a steam engine, are sixty feet long by a little under six feet diameter, and bear a torpedo on a spar at the bow. One of these struck a vessel last week, but for some reason the torpedo failed to explode, and the vessel struck never knew how near destruction she was. A torpedo boat with two engines it is supposed will make twelve to fourteen miles, and may, it seems to me, make attack in open daylight. I prefer a system which I have sketched, of boats armed with a 16-inch shell gun; the gun placed in the bow weighs eight or nine thousand pounds. One shell holding say 28 pounds of powder, would destroy any wooden ship. —The exchange of prisoners if kept up will soon give us large additions to our veteran troops—say 25,000. The exchanged prisoners were received with music and other demonstrations yesterday. The President went among them, and was received with great enthusiasm.—Weather clear but cool; gardening just beginning.

March 22nd. On Sunday afternoon we all went to the capitol square to see the returned prisoners, another lot of whom had just arrived,—over one thousand. We took along two small baskets of provisions and a demijon of cold tea —Jessie and Minnie each carried a basket and Willie the tea; Minnie a little basket of cakes. There was a great crowd, and we barely saw a few of the prisoners by penetrating thro' the mass. The President and General Smith[9] said a few words, and about dark the mass moved off to Camp Lee.—Grant has been made Lieutenant General at the North and has assumed command of all their armies.[10]

March 23rd. Wednesday. The heaviest fall of snow this winter began yesterday. It lies eight to ten inches deep. Maria is in utter despair at the renewal of winter which she so much dislikes. We four sat down quietly as tho' there were no war and played a game of euchre. Anticipation of reduced prices under the new currency is still entertained. The state of it is now deplorable: Flour $300 the barrel;

a shad costs $35.; turkey, $5 to $9 per pound; beef, $5 to $6; Eggs, $7; and so on. How the poor live is incomprehensible. Even meal sells at $30 per bushel.

March 25th. Good Friday. It is raining fast, and with the snow we shall have plenty of water in the river and plenty of mud in the roads,—a bad prospect for the Yankees.—Major Cary[11] dined with us today. He commands the Bellona Arsenal and foundry, and is one of my best officers. He has been good enough to send us four or five wild turkeys lately—a great addition to our bill of fare. Minnie is his especial pet, and he is her "sweetheart." Her airs with him are comical.—General Elzey has been relieved of command here and placed in charge of the "Maryland line," to be more fully organized, with headquarters at Staunton.—The message of Governor Brown of Georgia and the speech of Vice-President Stephens excite much remark, and are looked upon with general disfavor. The former denounces the suspension of the *habeas corpus*, and the latter speaks cold of the three great measures of the government—the H.C.,[12] the currency and the military bills.

March 27th. Easter Sunday. The morning is bright but a cool raw wind is blowing. It is just three years ago today since I sent in my resignation in the U. S. Service. Another year of hard struggling will, I hope, serve to consolidate this Confederacy, and establish its right to enter the family of nations. Then it will, I believe, rapidly recover from the wounds it has received.—I go to breakfast with Mr. and Mrs. Jones.

April 1st. The weather still continues raw, damp, rainy, chilly. It is raining tonight. We are alone again in our quarters, Bayne and his family having taken rooms on Main Street. Two families can rarely get along without some discontents in one house, and it is well that we have quietly broken in two—pleasantly. Bayne is the most amiable and best man to get along with I have ever known. Maria is a little more difficult to please, and is too fond of having her own way, to get along perfectly well with others. —There is no war news. The bad weather prevents all military operation; and there is no information as to the plans of the enemy. They openly threaten Richmond, but it is still believed their main attack will be in Georgia.—I saw today in the hands of General F. H. Lee the pocket memo book of Dahlgren, in which is a rough draft in pencil of his published address to his troops, differing a little here and there; and among other memoranda on another page: "Jeff Davis and his Cabinet must be killed on the spot."— Bragg's quick decided spirit is, I believe, felt here. His presence I have no doubt does good. Every one feels that he will *assist* the President in the conduct of military mat- ters.

April 4th. The news from Forrest today is very good. He attacked Union City on the 25th and took 450 prisoners, Paducah afterwards and captured it, but did not hold it, the small pox being prevalent. He returns about six hundred prisoners who are on the way to Demopolis. He states his loss at only 25 killed and wounded, while the Yankee ac- counts had made it as high as thirteen hundred!—It appears that the Yankees have succeeded in making their way some distance up the Red River, and were above Alexandria at last accounts. They captured about 250 of our men at Fort de Russy, near Alexandria, with a few pieces of artillery.—Grant appears to be with Meade's Army, and it really looks as tho' serious work were intended on this line.—The weather is still very bad—it snowed hard on the 2nd.—Bayne has moved to a house on the upper end of Main Street and we feel quite lonesome here. Mamma has gone to bed with a faceache, and it is time for me to follow.

April 7th. The weather has cleared up, and eight or ten days of such will make the roads passable.—Grant really

seems to intend operations against Richmond. It will, I
trust, prove the final test and discomfiture of the enemy.
I saw the President yesterday. He asked me whether the
proportion of artillery with the army was not too large—a
subject I had lately bro't to his attention in a paper—and
then desired me to have some portable mills for making
meal, constructed to carry with the army. Prices of food
are still exorbitant: flour, $1.50 per pound; potatoes, $50.00
per bushel; tea, $30.00, and so on. There is, I fear, real
suffering in many families. I feel chagrin at times that *we*
should be so well off. The funding and taxation have evidently had no effect. About 240 millions have been funded,
and that with the tax on the remainder (33 1-3 per cent)
reduces the volume of currency full one half. The five dollar
bills are now taken reluctantly and at a discount, as they
have only till July to run. It is a real financial bewilder-
ment. By the 1st of July matters will be somewhat arranged,
I hope.

April 8th. It is three years ago today since I took charge
of the Ordnance Department of the Confederate States, at
Montgomery—three years of constant work and applica-
tion. I have succeeded beyond my utmost expectations.
From being the worst supplied of the Bureaus of the War
Department it is now the best. Large arsenals have been
organized at Richmond, Fayetteville, Augusta, Charleston,
Columbus, Macon, Atlanta and Selma, and smaller ones at
Danville, Lynchburgh and Montgomery, besides other estab-
lishments. A superb powder mill has been built at Augusta,
the credit of which is due to Col. G. W. Rains. Lead smelting works were established by me at Petersburgh, and
turned over to the Nitre and Mining Bureau, when that
Bureau was at my request separated from mine. A cannon
foundry established at Macon for heavy guns, and bronze
foundries at Macon, Columbus, Ga., and at Augusta; a
foundry for shot and shell at Salisbury, N. C.; a large shop
for leather work at Clarksville, Va.; besides the Armories
here and at Fayetteville, a manufactory of carbines has been

built up here; a rifle factory at Ashville (transferred to Columbia, S. C.) ; a new and very large armory at Macon, including a pistol factory, built up under contract here and sent to Atlanta, and thence transferred under purchase to Macon; a second pistol factory at Columbus, Ga.;—All of these have required incessant toil and attention, but have borne such fruit as relieves the country from fear of want in these respects. Where three years ago we were not making a gun, a pistol nor a sabre, no shot nor shell (except at the Tredegar Works)—a pound of powder—we now make all these in quantities to meet the demands of our large armies. In looking over all this I feel that my three years of labor have not been passed in vain.—Mamma is again suffering; she is not at all well.—There is no news. The daily papers are carping at the renewal of exchanges thro', as they say, Beast Butler, the outlaw.

April 10th. It is reported that the enemy is landing troops at Newport News, or somewhere below on the James River—said to be Burnside's troops. It is very doubtful. If it be so we must get the ironclads, of which there are three nearly ready, to hold the course of the River. The heavy rains will prevent active military operations for some time to come. It is said that General Lee is anxious to attack Grant before he can be reinforced. This seems probable. As I have had today a telegram from him asking that the arms from Wilmington be hastened to him, I judge he is getting his troops ready to do work.—It is raining incessantly.— An arrangement to resume the exchange of prisoners, tho' not announced, has doubtless been made.

April 11th. There is nothing farther as to the reported movements of the enemy on the lower James. The floods have caused some destruction of bridges, etc., and apprehensions of injury to the canal are entertained. The river is higher than it has been since '47. There is much anxiety on the subject of food for the capital. It is said, on the authority of the assessors, that the population of Richmond

is now 130,000 against 50,000 three years ago. The increase
seems hardly credible. With proper energy in the use of
the railroads there is no doubt food can be bro't forward
from the South and troops and Capitol [*sic*] fed; but the
passenger trains must be interrupted for a time.—Bayne
is little pleased with his new chief, the Secretary of the
Treasury. Mr. Memminger treats others with rudeness, and
is, besides, dogmatical, narrowminded and slow. He places
every fresh paper at the bottom of his pile, and makes it
await its turn patiently without much regard to its importance. *His* time, and *his* method are more important
than any subject can possibly be! Whenever I leave Mr. M.
after an interview, I feel somehow as tho' I had been trying to do something very much out of the way, so injured
and *put upon* does he represent himself. He always assumes
a bristling defensive, and makes you appear to be on the
aggressive toward him. Mr. Seddon compares him to a dog
who, when a new dog enters his domain, runs alongside of
him erecting his bristles and curving his back!—Gold has
gone to 171 in Yankeeland—within one per cent of what
it was at its highest a little over a year ago.

April 24th. A brilliant feat of arms was done at Plymouth on Sunday, Monday and Tuesday. General Hoke, of
North Carolina, marched against it with about five thousand men and with the aid of an ironclad, just finished,
took it partly by storm. 2500 men were taken; two gunboats destroyed and one captured; 100,000 pounds of bacon
and one thousand barrels of flour; twenty-five guns (among
them one 200-pounder Parrott), and other spoils. The town
was surrounded with fortifications of which both ends
rested on the river (Roanoke). The water front was left
to be covered by their gunboats. As soon, therefore, as our
ironclad appeared and destroyed the boats, our troops landed and occupied the town taking the works in reverse. Some
of them were, however, very strong. The garrison was summoned to surrender, and, after some fighting, in which
one fort was carried with heavy loss on our side, it was

again summoned. General Wessels[13] now asked an interview, in the course of which he told General Hoke[14] that
the defences were comparatively intact, and that his government held its officers to a strict accountability. He could
not, therefore, surrender. General Hoke replied, in sub-
stance: "My force is as you must see adequate to the storm-
ing of your works. I shall storm them at any cost of life,
and I warn you that if you expect to save your men by
hoisting the white flag at the last moment you deceive yourself. After my troops surmount the defences no quarter
will be given. The laws of war will be exacted." The fighting recommenced and our men were thrown forward to assault, but now the Yankees were discovered coming out of
their works, first singly, then in squads and platoons, and
finally four hundred threw down their arms and gave themselves up, and then the main fort surrendered, and all the
works fell. *No negro soldiers were taken prisoners*; but
about three hundred were taken as laborers and put to
work; and an hour after the surrender were busy placing
the captured bacon, flour and other stores, on our boats to
be bro't up the river to Halifax. Our ironclad was fairly
hit three times by the shot of the 200-pounder Parrott,
which broke the outer layer of two-inch iron, and indented
the inner without breaking thro'. Farther news is expected
from the same expedition, which it is hoped may capture
Newbern.

April 25th. Went to service in the morning yesterday,
but instead of sitting thro' the sermon, I took the children
out during the singing of the hymn, and walked with them
in the Capital Square, which they enjoyed more than they
could the sermon.—No farther news from General Hoke
and the Newbern expedition.—General Beauregard is at
Weldon. He has been assigned to the immediate command
it seems in that quarter, the limits of his command having
been extended.—News of an advance by Lee is every day
expected. Our troops are in excellent condition but the
cavalry is not yet all to the front.—News of Yankee dis-

aster up the Red River is gradually being confirmed, but without sufficient distinctness. They confess to a loss of two thousand killed, wounded and missing. We claim now seven thousand prisoners and nineteen pieces of artillery. The Yankee General Ransom, commanding their cavalry,[15] is reported by them wounded.—A good deal of excitement is created by the moving away of the lady *note signers* to Columbia. It was proposed to move the chief portion of each department leaving only the chiefs, and such as were neces- sary to the business of the army. This would have been very embarrassing to us. It has since been reconsidered. The object is, of course, to diminish the number of mouths here, the question of feeding General Lee's army and the Capital being a very critical one.

April 26th. The weather is now beautiful, and very favorable to military operations. The news is that a large force is landing at Yorktown, and that an early advance may be expected against this place from that direction. It is still doubtful where the enemy will endeavor to strike the heaviest blow, here or in Georgia. Our armies are maintained in full force at both places. Johnston has about forty thousand men, and Lee, with Longstreet, full 55,000. It is supposed that Lee will take the initiative immediately. That he has not done so is, I suppose, because all his cavalry and artillery is not yet to the front.—The problem of the currency is a curious one. We have stricken out of existence 500,000,000 of dollars of currency, yet prices have not receded. It is evident that parties holding food and sup- plies mean, for the present, to hold on to them. There will thus be a scarcity of money, yet high prices. Until the farmers are forced by taxation to sell their produce it is possible these prices may continue. It is now better to buy with gold, when gold can be commanded. Eggs can be had for 12 1-2 cents in gold, while they cost $6.00 in currency. I have ceased to draw my pay, and am determined to live on the sale of such things as I can spare. General Sam Jones has been assigned to command at Charleston, and General

Robert Ransom to Richmond. General Hoke is a Major General for his capture of Plymouth.

Friday, April 29th. There seems to be no longer reason to doubt that General E. K. Smith met the 13th Army Corps on the 8th at some point on the west side of the upper Red River, and defeated it with heavy loss—say four thousand men in killed, wounded and missing; and twenty pieces of artillery.[16] The Yankees claim that General A. J. Smith came up next day, and drove back our forces with loss, recapturing some of the artillery. It is probable, therefore, the enemy have been beaten before they could unite their forces, and that the second column simply saved the remains of the first from destruction. At all events the Red River expedition is frustrated and Louisiana safe.—I had a short conference with General Bragg yesterday. His views are so startling and decided that I am tempted to think him a *little cracked.* The subject was the removal of machinery and operatives from here on account of scarcity of food. He said movements would begin in a few weeks which would compel people to leave to escape starvation, as all food would be taken by the troops; "it is probable that the town will be *pillaged* by our own men for want of ability to supply them," meaning when the railroads should be cut about Richmond.

April 30th. The indications are now that Burnside's Corps may reinforce Grant it having gone to Washington from Annapolis; there can be little doubt, I suppose that a powerful army is collecting in front of Lee. His army is as large, perhaps larger than it was a year ago when it defeated Hooker; but then he had Jackson.—I saw the President yesterday, having succeeded in making a corn-mill for him, which is to be used with the troops. He was much pleased at the specimen of meal made by it; and added that everybody to whom he had imparted his views as to getting up a corn-mill of this sort, "had told him how and why it could not be done, but that I had shown how it could be done." Possibly I ought to be master miller in place of Chief of Ordnance.—Congress meets day after tomorrow (Monday).

Sunday, May 1st. We attended this afternoon the funeral of one of the President's little boys, (Joe), who was killed yesterday evening by a fall from the back piazza. No one saw the poor little fellow fall, and he probably had been lying some little time when he was found. His legs were both broken and his head fractured. It is a very sad thing to see a fine healthy child, gamboling about yesterday, and today carried along in his little coffin. The President is very much attached to his children, and very caressing toward them, and this is a heavy sorrow to him. Last winter I once saw him take this little fellow off to hear him say his prayers as he went to bed.

May 2nd. News today that Washington, N. C., is in our hands, having been evacuated by the enemy. Should we now be able to reduce Newbern the waters of North Carolina would again be in our possession, and the series of reverses, beginning with the fall of Fort Hatteras, would be redeemed. The recent battles on the Red River seem to have taken place on the 8th and 9th of April. The Yankees report General Mouton as certainly killed.[17] As yet we have no authentic advices from Confederate sources. Two Yankee gunboats and three transports are reported at West Point. The great scene of the drama of this year, perhaps the last one of this war (joyful tho't), must soon open. The omens are all good for us. Thus far military events have been in our favor.

May 4th. The enemy are reported to have crossed the Rappahannock at Ely's Ford, and to have advanced to the old ground, near Chancellorville. The crossing may be only a reconnaissance in force.—Rode out yesterday to attend the trial of the siege 8-inch gun, and the 9-pounder light gun. The first was found spiked by the accidental breaking of a gimlet in the vent. A charge fired from the muzzle failed to drive the vent clear. The trial with this gun had, therefore, to be postponed. The 9-pounder did very well and gave very fair ranges. I had a brisk ride out and back and feel quite shaken. The day was clear and cool, wind cool. The fortifications on the Manchester side are very strong and well built.

May 5th. The enemy, it is ascertained, have landed in some force on the north side of the James River, below Westover. Thirty-four transports are reported.—No farther news of movements on the Rapidan. Troops are coming in from the South as far as Charleston. From Savannah and points farther south they are ordered to Dalton, so that Johnston ought now to have an army of nearly 60,000 including his cavalry. The great points of collision are evidently here and with Johnston's army.—There are advices here from Shreveport to the 12th of April. There can be no doubt of the serious defeat of Banks, and his withdrawal to Alexandria, and perhaps to the Mississippi.

May 6th. The enemy crossed at Ely's and Germania [Germanna] Fords on the 4th, and were met on the 5th by Ewell's and Hill's Corps, the former on the old turnpike, the latter on the plank road. They were repulsed at both points with a loss of four guns and "many prisoners." General J. M. Jones, (my classmate), was killed, and General Stafford mortally wounded.[18] Our loss is apparently heavy.

Today the fight was renewed, but there is no news of definite character, except that all is going on well. General Jenkins, of South Carolina, is reported mortally wounded, and General Longstreet severely wounded in the shoulder, both by their own men, (Mahone's Brigade).[19] 1200 prisoners are reported as having arrived at Orange C. H.—The effort appears to have been to turn Lee's right.—A large force has landed on City Point and marched toward the Railroad, but at latest accounts had not yet cut it. This ef-

fort, commanded by W. F. Smith, is doubtless aimed at
Drury's Bluff. An enemy's gunboat was blown up on the
river by a torpedo, and entirely destroyed. The forces here
are adequate to holding the defences of Richmond, and if
General Lee is successful against Grant's attack, no fears
need be entertained.—General Beauregard is at Petersburg
by this time with three brigades, besides some troops of
Pickett's.—The enemy is reported advancing in Western
Virginia to destroy the Salt Works. At Chattanooga the
enemy is also reported moving, tho' slowly.—One of the
officers on duty here came to me at midnight to say that
his brother, Colonel I. Thompson Brown, was killed in the
fight today, (6th), and desired leave which was of course
given him. Colonel Brown is well known and a great favorite in Richmond. When will these terrible things come to
an end.—Captain Hutter,[20] stationed at Danville, stays with
us tonight. The weather is beautiful, and the day has been
quite warm. The stars are looking down upon many a poor
wounded man lying in pain, and on the mangled corpses of
many thousand brave men.

May 8th. No farther official news of the fight of the
5th. On the 6th General Lee reports our troops thrown into
momentary confusion by the attack of the enemy on the
Divisions of Hill, which were being relieved by fresh troops.
As soon as the troops got in position they recovered the
ground which had been lost, and then attacking the enemy's
left drove it off the field, leaving its killed and wounded,
and forcing it back to its position behind the Brooke Road,
where it is entrenched. Rumors are rife of farther successes. Our killed are not many, but a good many wounded,
the fight having been in a wooded country with musketry.
Fighting has been going on during the day (7th), below the
Petersburgh road, where the farther progress of the enemy
is disputed by our forces—by this time, I hope, twelve or
fifteen thousand. It is stated they are entrenching. Another
gunboat has been sunk or destroyed, having been captured
by the men of Hunton's[21] Brigade.—Beauregard is probably

at Petersburg, tho' he was ill at Weldon on the 6th.—Reports believed to be authentic state that Price has captured the greater part of Steele's command.[22] The ironclad "Albemarle" returned to Plymouth after having had a fight of 48 hours (?) with gunboats. She broke the muzzle off her after gun.[23]—We are preparing to move our carbine factory with all the operatives and their families, to Tallassee, Ala.[24]

May 10th. On yesterday morning a dispatch from General Lee reported that General R. H. Anderson had met the enemy at Spotsylvania C. H. and repulsed one Army Corps (Warren's), and a Division of Cavalry, "with heavy slaughter." Receiving reinforcements the enemy renewed the attack and was again "handsomely repulsed."

, On the 6th Gordon's Brigade attacked the extreme right of the enemy and drove it, forcing him to abandon his communications by Germanna Ford. In this fight Major General Seymour and Brigadier General Shaler[25] were captured. The enemy afterwards took up his bridges and withdrew toward Fredericksburgh, our columns keeping parallel to his march. In this movement the collision at Spotsylvania C. H. took place. The body of General Jenkins, of South Carolina, was taken to the Capitol yesterday evening, and General Stafford was buried in Hollywood in the forenoon.—The day was one of excitement;—in the morning it was reported the enemy had reached Chester, on the Railroad between here and Petersburg, and that they were fighting at Drury's Bluff. Later news showed that this was incorrect, and that the attack was directed toward Petersburg. All the local forces were called out, alarm bells rung, etc. At night, news of a raid at Beaver Dam, on the Central Railroad, again caused excitement. It is reported this morning that the enemy was driven from there by the local cavalry.

Evening. The news is bad from Western Virginia. Brigadier General Jenkins' Cavalry command was attacked by a Yankee force and defeated. Dublin Depot is now in pos-

session of the enemy.[26] Colonel McCausland,[27] said to be a
very good officer, is in temporary command at New River.
It is hoped that Morgan and W. E. Jones may restore our
fortunes in that quarter. There is no definite news from
Lee. Fighting has doubtless been going on, but the result
is unknown.—Yesterday a party of Yankee Cavalry—
estimated at a thousand—took possession of the Central
Railroad at Beaver Dam, capturing three trains laden with
commissary stores, including over 200,000 pounds of bacon.
This is a very serious loss at this moment.—This morning
there was fighting in the vicinity of Drury's Bluff, General
Ransom having advanced with two Brigades—Gracie's and
Barton's[28]—and attacked the enemy. The affair was done
to attract the enemy from Petersburg, and resulted in a
loss of about 150 of Barton's brigade. Gracie was not engaged. The affair was, I judge, unfavorable to us. Troops
are concentrating at P. [Petersburg]. Everybody com-
plains of the tardiness of Beauregard's movements. The
woods are on fire where the fight took place today and the
horizon is lined with fires tonight in that direction.—Hoke
has, it is said, relieved Pickett at P. Pickett is very dissipated, it is asserted.—I hope all will go well.—People look
very anxious as well they may with thirty thousand
Yankees close upon the city, and not twelve thousand troops
here to defend it.

Wednesday, May 11th. The day has been one of the
greatest excitement. I slept but a few hours last night
having been called up by messages, and kept awake by the
ringing of alarm bells and the blowing of alarm whistles
the most of the night. At five this morning I went to Mr.
Seddon's office and found him laboring under the impression that the last hours of Richmond were at length numbered.—The entire cavalry force of Meade's army were
reported to be rapidly approaching the devoted city from
the direction of Ashland, with Stuart at their heels it is
true, but having a good deal the start of him. All the city
militia were transferred to that side of the city, and a bri-

gade of old troops (Hunton's), from Chaffin's Farm.—We
breathe more freely now (11:00 p.m.), as Stuart is on their
flank and the city defences in their front. It is hoped, therefore, that they may be worsted if not caught.—As all my
officers and clerks are in the field I am obliged to attend
to details myself and have trudged about the streets until
I am thoroughly tired.—The news from General Lee shows
that there has been sharp fighting on the 9th and 10th, the
enemy being continually, and, as it appears, easily repulsed.
Still the enemy shows a bold front, and makes desperate
assaults on Lee's position, which appears to extend from
Spotsylvania C. H., on the right, to Shady Grove church, on
the left. General Hayes and Walker[29] are reported wounded
yesterday. How this continued fighting will end cannot yet
be predicted. If supplies do not fail I have no doubt of Lee's
ability to maintain himself. Meantime the attack on Richmond from the large force landed at Bermuda Hundred is
repelled by the forces now under Beauregard; and he is to
take the offensive tomorrow, and drive them to their gunboats. He has now, all told, a force of fully sixteen thousand
men. The three ironclads will be ready to partake in the
conflict as soon as they can get thro' the obstructions, (the
"Richmond," the "Virginia" and the "Fredericksburgh").
I fear they are too vulnerable to the heavy guns of the
monitors, of which there are four.—In the fighting with
the cavalry force today Colonel H. Clay Pate was killed,
and our cavalry had to give back before the superior forces
of the enemy, who number about five thousand, it is said.
Stuart has about 2,500.

May 13th. Richmond is again breathing freely for the
moment. After severe fighting at the Yellow Church,[30] in
which Stuart was mortally wounded about 2:30 p.m., on
Wednesday, and after some skirmishing yesterday, the
enemy at last retired by Mechanicsville, without any serious
loss. There is much dissatisfaction at this result. The enemy
were, however, very strong, say eight thousand; still with
three veteran brigades and a large force of "locals" some-

thing might perhaps have been done more than was done.
—On the south side the enemy yesterday crossed the Petersburgh Railroad and went to the Coal Pits, on the Danville
road, cutting that and doing some other damage. Troops
have been sent after him. It is tho't that General Hoke is
to attack the enemy tomorrow in some force.—A courier
brings dispatches from Lee, which are, I fear, very unfavorable. He has been forced out of his lines on the left, and
Major General Johnson and Brig-General Stewart captured,[31] losing besides a good deal of artillery. The courier,
poor fellow, knew nothing of our misfortunes, and was re-
tailing gay stories of recent successes, which will be detailed
in the morning papers no doubt.

May 14th. The enemy has effected little damage to the
Danville Road, and it is again in running order. Trains also
left today for General Lee on the Central Railroad. So the
city is again free for the time being, but I have little confidence in its remaining so long. Our enemy is here in very
great force and will harass us in every possible way. The
newspaper despatches from General Lee's army, are rather
favorable to us, but I expect to hear that he is falling back.
In truth I see no solution of our defence of Richmond,
except in this: to concentrate all our forces here, and keep
open communications with the city.—Heavy firing has been
going on to the right of Drury's Bluff all day, with some
casualties to us. Beauregard is there, and I hope the troops
are sufficient for an attack on the enemy.

May 15th. The despatches, from General Lee and his
principal officers, are quite hopeful. Still he has lost two
thousand prisoners and twenty guns.—The loss of the
enemy in the struggle of Thursday must have been enormous. An officer, who was in the fight, describes the attacking force to have come up in line after line, ten in number;
and to have been mown down by our artillery in heaps. The
"Herald" of the 12th states the minimum loss of Grant, in

the fights of the first week, to be 27,000 killed, wounded and missing. At that rate their losses must now sum up nearly 50,000. Ours cannot exceed 15,000. They have lost seven general officers, killed and wounded—Sedgwicke[32] is certainly killed. I knew him very well at Old Point Comfort. —A fight occurred yesterday in which we took three hundred prisoners and four colors. General Lee does not ask for reinforcements, but for supplies of provisions, tho' he is in no danger of starvation as the country behind him still affords supplies.—Lieutenant-Colonel Baldwin,[33] his chief Ordnance officer, reports his ammunition holding out very well—one hundred rounds yet per man, of small arm ammunition. Supplies are again going forward.—On the South Side of James River, we have beaten the enemy off at the Appomattox bridge, and restored the Danville Railroad. General Beauregard is preparing an attack in force, and ought to have full twenty thousand men. General Whiting has joined him from Wilmington. Firing has been going on all day, chiefly artillery, with some skirmishing. We could see smoke of the guns and the bursting of shells from the cupola of the War Department. Willie saw and watched it with interest. A flag of truce was sent up to Curl's Neck by the enemy, for what purpose is not known. Sheridan's cavalry is said to rest from its fights about Richmond, about Malvern, and may again resume its raid after a brief repose.—In Western Virginia Averell has certainly been defeated by Morgan, Jones and Jackson, and is said to be lying wounded at Christiansburg a prisoner.[34] I *hope* this may be true.—For the past week it has been raining every day.—If we could receive fifteen thousand men from Johnston's army, as we ought to, all would soon be well. If Johnston had the happy inspiration that Desaix had at Marengo, he would send here one of his corps, without waiting for orders; as the enemy is evidently not to attack him and he must have 65,000 men idly waiting there, while the roar of battle thunders over a dozen battle fields in Virginia and the fate of the nation is being decided here.

May 16th. A severe engagement took place on the South
Side today, beginning at early light, between the forces of
General Beauregard and that of Butler. We began the attack and drove the enemy, capturing a Brigadier General,
(Heckman),[35] with his staff and over a thousand prisoners.
Seven pieces of artillery, and many of the horses are reported captured. Our losses are not reported, but are said
to be heavy in Gracie's brigade, and in the Washington
(N. C.) Artillery. At 5:00 o'clock Beauregard despatched
that he was preparing to renew the attack and hoped to
effect a junction with Whiting, who was at Walthall Junction. The enemy is to the east of the railroad, about the
half-way house.—I have had great trouble to get ammunition for the Enfield arms, the troops having come up from
North Carolina with only forty rounds.

Breckinridge has met and driven back Sigel in the valley with considerable loss, and in some confusion.[36] He is
retiring behind the Shenandoah, burning the bridges.

The news from Johnston is that the enemy is in line
in front of him, and on the 14th two attacks of his were
repelled.—General Lee says the enemy still moves toward
our right, apparently with the view of flanking, but has
not renewed his attack since Thursday.

People look quite hopeful today. I hope their hearts are
grateful to the brave fellows who are standing between us
and our enemies, and pouring out their blood for our safety. I think of it every hour in the day with gratitude and
sorrow for the noble fellows, who never flinch nor falter
before the enemy.

May 17th. Our losses yesterday were quite heavy,
amounting, I fear, to quite two thousand in killed, wounded
and missing. It was Barton's Brigade (commanded by General Fry) which it seems suffered chiefly. Hagood's[37] (S.C.)
also lost heavily, eighteen men being killed in one company.
We captured quite fifteen hundred prisoners, and five
pieces of artillery—one regiment from Springfield, Mass.,
commanded by a Colonel Lee,[38] was captured almost entire.

The enemy have fallen back to their lines extending from the James River to the Appomattox, about three miles long, strongly defended, and, of course, supported by the gun-boats. It is rumored tonight that they are crossing some troops to the north side below Chaffin's Farm, communicating, no doubt, with Sheridan, whose cavalry is still about Malvern Hills.

No fighting above, the enemy still extending to the left and taking position behind the Ni River. General Lee will, I suppose occupy the range of heights south of the same river—his right just in front of Guinea's station.—The road to Petersburgh is again cleared of the enemy, and may soon again be placed in running order. It is also repaired south of Petersburgh.—Spent the evening at Mrs. Jones, meeting Mr. Lyon, Mrs. Marye, Colonel Baldwin,[39] (M.C.), and Mr. and Mrs. Miles (S.C.).[40]

May 20th. One of the victims of the fight of Monday lies in our house—Lieutenant Robert M. Taft, of Charleston. The poor fellow, whose family we know very well, sent for me on Tuesday at noon, but, owing to some stupidity, I did not receive the message until late at night, after his death. It will be a sad blow to his poor mother who is a very fond mother.—There are reports of another fight below, and that Beauregard attacked and drove the enemy out of their rifle pits. I know the ambulance committee of Richmond was sent for today to Chester Station.—My heart sickens at the thought of another day of slaughter like that of Monday. There is little doubt, it seems, that if General Whiting had performed the part allotted to him by Beauregard on Monday, the Yankee army would have suffered a severe defeat. He has been relieved from command at Petersburgh in consequence.—I saw the President today; he was in better spirits than I have seen him in for a long time, and told several anecdotes, en passant. One of General Taylor in Mexico, who in passing by a soldier lying by the wayside during a fight, accosted him: "My poor fellow where were you wounded." "I'm not exactly wounded,

General, but—" "Yes, and taking good care that you won't be, you d—d rascal," said the indignant General, when he found it was one who was skulking.

The President called for an aide, and Colonel Wood came in. "But," said the President, smiling, "I want a *writing* aide." "Then I'll call Colonel Ives,"[41] said Colonel Wood, blushing a little, but good natured. "Never mind," said the President, "You'll do, I was jesting. And to relieve you from any embarrassment, I will tell you a little anecdote of General Jackson.[42] There was an officer by the name of Captain Bean appointed from the Rangers to the 1st Dragoons. He could not write his name, but had learned to sign his name 'Capt. B., Capt. Rangers,' and when he was transferred to the Dragoons he continued the signature as before. Colonel Kearney[43] went to General Jackson and told him: 'Capt. B. is too illiterate for an officer; he cannot even write.' The old General threw up his specks and said: 'Can't write! eh! Well, he fought with me at —— Springs, and I know he made *his mark!*' "

The story is somewhat old but did very well under the circumstances, and Colonel Wood went on to write a letter to General Beauregard from the Presidential dictation.

May 21st. The fight yesterday drove the enemy nearer to their gunboats, but cost us four or five hundred in killed and wounded. General W. S. Walker,[44] commanding Evans' Brigade, is missing, supposed captured. The enemy today evince no design of moving away down the river. The number of transports is reported at seventy. The enemy again cut the Central Railroad at Hanover C. H., but have been forced off. It is said they are all about the other side of the Chickahominy, about Mechanicsville, plundering and destroying. It is reported that the negro troops on the Peninsula are committing the most revolting excesses. Our cavalry force is not adequate to driving them away and keeping them off. It is heartrending to hear of the maltreatment of the inhabitants.—No news of fighting in General Lee's army.—General Johnston is falling back as hard as he can and has placed himself behind the Etowah River with his headquarters at Altoona. It is surmised that he will reach Macon in a few days at the rate he is retreating. —I trust the country will sooner or later find out what sort of a general he is. I don't think he will suit the emergency.

Sunday, May 22nd. Listened to a very long and very tiresome sermon this morning in St. Paul's, from an old clergyman. He must have preached over an hour.—General Lee has his headquarters at Hanover C. H., with Hill's Corps—the others following him. The movement of Grant down the Mattaponi renders this necessary. It is probable that Grant is seeking to unite with Butler. No farther news from Johnston, and nothing from Beauregard.—Hugh arrived today with a part of his regiment.—There are nearly five thousand cavalry here, and on their way here from the South.

May 23rd. No items of news of any interest.—With the cavalry now arriving here there will, I think, be no difficulty in keeping open our communications.—It is said that the body of Grant's army is at Bowling Green and Milford Depot.—A few heavy guns have been heard today in the direction of Drury's Bluff, but it has not transpired what they meant.

May 25th. Yesterday we heard that the enemy had crossed the North Anna, at three different points, and fighting had begun at Hanover Junction, the operator having left as he wrote the dispatch.

A great battle must be fought today then on the ground directly south of the N. Anna, extending from Jericho Ford to beyond the Junction. I cannot but think that Lee is as well prepared to fight now as he ever will be. He is nearly as strong as when he breasted the first shock of battle at Wilderness, having been reinforced by six brigades from here, and by Breckinridge's division from the valley, they

having joined him after defeating Sigel at Newmarket. I
suppose Lee's strength to be sixty thousand. Grant may still
be able to muster 85,000 to 90,000 men, if the reports of
his original strength are not exaggerated. We have, therefore, reduced the disparity of numbers very greatly, and
ought to hope for Grant's defeat, without presumption. The
rapidity of his movements indicates strength and confidence. Today or tomorrow will tell the tale of defeat to us,
or of disaster and ruin to him. We can still fall back upon
our intrenchments; but Grant is irretrievably ruined if
defeated. He has never before ventured so far from his
gunboats.—It is said our ironclads are getting out thro'
the obstructions. I fear they will never get back again.—
Johnston verifies all our predictions of him. He is falling
back just as fast as his legs can carry him. As I did him
wrong in underestimating the strength of the force in front
of him, I hope he will also vindicate himself still farther
by beating them in spite of our predictions. He is falling
back behind the Chattahoochie, and will, I fear, give up
Atlanta. The Chattahoochie can be "flanked" as well as
any position he has held, and it is this process which is
driving him back. Where he will stop Heaven only knows.

May 26th. No fighting seems to have occurred yesterday. Grant pauses before he trusts himself beyond the North
Anna. He does well to collect his strength before the peri-
lous advance, from which, I hope, he is never to return
without a *thorough* defeat—for defeated he is already, if
a general who makes an unsuccessful attack and recoils
from his adversary can be said to be defeated.—Our position appears to be behind the North Anna, immediately in
front of Hanover Junction. General Lee is understood to
have left bridges and boats on the North Anna after crossing it. This may have given Grant pause, tho' a part of his
army is understood to have crossed.—No definite news of
Johnston's position. The Atlanta papers continue to assert
that he is "master of the situation"—a meaningless phrase
copied from Yankee papers.—A week ago the new ironclad

"Raleigh" crossed the bar at Wilmington and drove off the blockaders without, however, doing any mischief. In retiring she got aground inside and is lost. Such is the fate of the Navy under its present administration. Our three ironclads here are now below the obstruction. I fear they will next be lost, tho' care will, I think, be taken not to venture down too far.

May 27th. Skirmishing yesterday only at Hanover Junction, and some artillery firing. Reinforcements are still going forward to General Lee. No doubt both sides are preparing for the final struggle. Defeat will indeed be woe to us!—According to accounts from Atlanta General Johnston's position is not a bad one, and all there feel confident of success yet in that campaign, unpromising as its beginning is.

A heavy battery is to be placed in position at Howlett's Farm, below Drury's Bluff, with a view of annoying the enemy's shipping. Two 8-inch rifles (one captured) are to be placed in position, and five 10-inch Columbiads.—The body of Lieutenant Taft has been with us since last Wednesday, and leaves today for Charleston in charge of his brother Walter. His grief last night at closing the box containing the metal coffin, which has been lying in my little *study,* was very touching, my wife says.—Yesterday I heard of the somewhat unexpected death of my old friend and classmate, Major Smith Stansbury.[45] He died at Halifax, N. S., on the 26th. He and I were always side by side in our classes, and I had hoped much from his assistance in this war. His mind was of the highest order.

May 27th. Evening. Grant is known to have recrossed such of his troops as were south of the North Anna, and to be crossing the Pamunky [*sic*] at Hanover town. Lee is making corresponding changes and was at Ashland this morning. Whether he will strike Grant between the Chickahominy and the Pamunky [*sic*] remains to be seen. Such was doubtless his intention, but he may have reconsidered it and

conclude to occupy the lines this side of the C.—No official
information from Johnston.—Bragg is bitterly assaulted
in two journals this morning, without much harm done.[46]
—I walked up to Capitol Square this morning, where the
"Cadets" of the Lexington School were being reviewed by
General Bragg. They moved very well. A flag was pre-
sented by Governor Smith, and a speech made to them by
Mr. Bocock in presenting the resolution of thanks passed
by Congress.[47]

May 29th. General Lee was yesterday at Atlee's Station
on the Central Railroad. Grant's position was not exactly
known. He was supposed to be bearing toward West Point,
perhaps facilitating a junction with Butler, who, it was said
yesterday, was striking his tents. If so our battery at
Howlett's will be too late.—No official news from Johnston.
—From the Red River we hear that Banks has escaped with
most of his army and fleet. The latter was saved by building
a dam across the river below the falls and then raising the
water so that the vessels could float out over the rapids
where they had been caught by the low water. If *our* boats
had been so caught we would simply have blown them up.

Gold has risen at New York to 186. When Grant began
his movements it was 171.—The weather is quite cool
enough for a little fire.—Provisions are coming in somewhat more freely. Trains laden with corn are constantly
arriving. The fear of starvation has, therefore, nearly sub-
sided. Four vessels have arrived thro' the blockade at W.
[Wilmington].

June 1st. I have been quite indisposed for the past three
days.—The army is now in position from about Atlee's
Station on the left to Cold Harbor on the right. The enemy's
line extends from the Central Road to Dispatch Station on
the York River. Heavy firing was going on this morning,
and a general engagement may be bro't on any day, or any
hour. General Lee has been quite indisposed with bilious
dysentery, but is able to be out again.—General Breckin-

ridge appears to be rising in favor as a dashing commander.
A. P. Hill does not sustain himself.—Early is looked upon
as one of the best leaders.

Yesterday there appears to have been an assault on the
enemy's lines at Bethesda Church, in which we lost heavily
—four field officers killed and wounded, three mortally.
It was Pegram's brigade led by Colonel Willis which suffered so seriously.[48] Some prisoners were taken by us.—
Beauregard's forces have been moved chiefly to the north
side, Butler having drawn off most, if not all of his forces,
probably to West Point.—No news of interest from Johnston, who still appears to maintain his position west of
Marietta.

11:00 P.M. No general engagement today beyond the
Chickahominy, despite appearances to the contrary.—Hugh
went out toward Atlee's Station with a portion of his regiment. So many cavalry officers have been killed in the last
few fights that we parted from him with a feeling of gloom.
I hope all will turn out well with him.—Beauregard is still
on the Southside confronting Butler, tho' rumor had assigned him to General Lee.

June 2nd. There was some fighting yesterday between
McLaw's and Anderson's divisions, and the enemy on the
right; and Breckinridge on the left, the latter capturing
150 prisoners. The general engagement still appears to be
delayed, however; tho' from the circumstances that the local
forces are called out and sent to Bottom's Bridge, I judge
the final dispositions are made. Should the day be favorable we may hear the roar of artillery in the morning.—
Our ironclads have as yet made nothing out of their passage
thro' the obstructions. They appear to treat the enemy with
distant respect.—It has been raining freely since 5:00 P.M.

June 4th. Rode out to the battlefield yesterday afternoon, returning about 9:00 P.M. A heavy fight had taken
place in the forenoon and a field to the front was covered

with dead Yankees. Our casualties were very small, amounting to but two in one of the brigades engaged. We (Major Merlin and myself) had scant time for observation as the enemy sharpshooters, about seven hundred yards distant, were evidently taking aim at us, and several balls struck close by. Met A. P. Hill as we were coming away. Said he was arranging for a little expedition to drive the enemy from a position. We heard sharp firing after we got six or seven miles away—doubtless this expedition. Our troops were lying behind triple lines of breastworks. They have acquired quite a respect for this sort of entrenchment, and work like beavers when they take up a new position. They began the war with a contempt for the spade, but now thoroughly believe in it. They use bayonets, tin pans, and even, I am told, split their tin canteens to get a utensil that will throw up earth.—Met General Lee near the field, with the President. The General kindly stopped and beckoned me to him, cautioning me not to go near the lines as I might be shot, with my blue cape, by either side; would rather, he added in half jocular way, that I would return and send him ammunition. I agreed to send him a Whitworth gun, which I did as soon as I got back. All were in excellent spirits, and agreed that the Yankees' loss that morning must have been enormous.—The weather is beautiful, clear and not too warm—nights cool.—It is Minnie's birthday— five years old. I have just given her a little book like this and wrote her name "Christine Amelia" on it, which seems to make her quite as happy as an elaborate present.

June 5th. There has been a good deal of rain, tho' not very violent, and military operations have been somewhat slack. There is a report that a portion of Breckinridge's line was broken thro' last night and that we lost a good many men. I have not been able to get anything authentic. The "Herald" of the 1st has a ridiculous report from Butler saying that a meeting had been held in this city, at which the giving up or burning of the city was discussed—that the Mayor (Mr. Mayo) [49] was in favor of sur-

rendering and had in consequence been arrested and thrown
into Castle Thunder!—The enemy appears to be established
on the Chickahominy, opposite Bottom's Bridge, within
sharpshooting distance of our troops on this side.

June 6th. The morning is beautiful—would it were as
peaceful as it is lovely. What have we done that the Almighty should scourge us with such a war—so relentless
and so repugnant.—There apparently was no fighting
yesterday. Grant seems inclined to try a passage of the
Chickahominy at Bottom's Bridge. What good that would
do him is the question. It brings him farther from instead
of nearer to Richmond. He is now as near as he ever will
be, I trust. Getting over to Butler and taking Petersburgh
from *below* City Point might *annoy* us, but would hardly
advance his object. I think he is at his wit's end.

June 7th. The report is that Grant has withdrawn his
forces from our left front. It is not known what his movements are but suspected to be to the south side, at some of
the lower bridges over the Chickahominy.

The painful news of the defeat and death of General
W. E. Jones was received yesterday.[50] He met Hunter's
forces at Mount Hope, about seven miles from Staunton
and fell early in the fight. Staunton appears to be in possession of the enemy, and it is rumored they are also at
Lexington. Jones was a graduate of the Class of '48, and
a very good cavalry officer. He was known as Grumble
Jones, from his grumbling disposition and manner.—Breckinridge probably goes to the valley in command today. He
was bruised by a cannon ball which passed thro' his home.
—I saw the President yesterday in reference to a bill for
increasing the number of Ordnance officers. He objected
to a proviso in the bill which gave preference in the appointments to persons already acting as officers in the field. He
construed this into an interference with Executive preroga-
tive, and showed more sensitiveness than seemed becoming
to appointments of officers of such inferior grades.—The

capture of the U. S. steamer "Water Witch" near Savannah, by boarding, seems a bold and brilliant affair. We lost the Lieutenant (Pelot)[51] in command and three men killed.

June 9th. I have been suffering greatly from neuralgia in the face for some days; and yesterday suffered intensely, until relieved by a dose of opium and quinine. This gave me pleasant dreams or hallucinations all night long. No news from any direction.—Grant apparently does nothing.— Breckinridge is opposing the farther advances of the enemy at Meacham's River. Affairs look to me more and more critical. I cannot see where farther reinforcements are to come from.—Lee is waiting and Grant is gathering strength here. The same appears to be the condition of things at Atlanta. Johnston is waiting while Sherman is receiving reinforcements. What the issue will be is in God's hands— nothing but an unforeseen event can, it seems to me, save us from the gradually rising strength of our opponents; or rather from the defeats our waning strength must entail. Our losses here all told are about 25,000 men, killed, wounded and captured, in Lee's Army alone, and perhaps five thousand on the South side. Where can we supply such a waste of men? We can hold out in all else. Lee's strength altogether is about five thousand less than when he first met Grant at the Wilderness, say fifty thousand infantry; his cavalry is now larger.

Monday, June 13th. I have suffered severely with "face-ache" since Thursday. It left me suddenly last night but the medicine I have taken makes me feel badly.—There is no change in General Lee's situation. The enemy attacked Petersburgh on Friday in some force, and were finally repulsed. The militia lost about ten killed, or mortally wounded, and about 27 wounded. They fought very staunchly, but were overpowered before the reinforcements arrived. It is said their stubborn resistance saved the town. —The battle at New Hope was a severe disaster to us, resulting in the loss of some 1500 in killed, wounded and captured, and in the capture of a great many of our sick and wounded at Staunton, which was entered by Hunter on Monday last. He was joined here by Crook and Averell, making an aggregate force of about fourteen thousand. The loss of the battle at New Hope is attributed to the giving way of the 60th Virginia Regiment. General Jones is said to have lost his life in the attempt to rally them. The troops then fell back to Waynesboro, saving all their artillery and trains. The enemy's advance is said to be within 25 miles of Lynchburgh, and to be in possession of Lexington.— The news from the north is that Lincoln and Andrew Johnson were nominated at Baltimore by the convention which met on the 7th; and that gold was 194 1-2 on the 8th—a very satisfactory commentary.

Wednesday, June 15th. We heard yesterday of the wounding of Hugh (commanding 6th S.C. Cavalry) at the fight at Louisa C. H. on Saturday. He was shot thro' the left breast, the ball coming out at the edge of the shoulder blade. After being placed in an ambulance the train was captured by a dash of a Yankee brigade in the rear of General Hampton. After being four or five hours in possession of the enemy, he was again recaptured by the cavalry of Fitz Lee, and is now at the house of Mr. Hunter, at Louisa, doing quite well. Saw today Captain Gregg of his regiment, who was shot thro' the right arm at the same time, also captured and re-captured. Hampton has whipped Sheridan pretty thoroughly and sent him over to Fredericksburgh. Early, with Ewell's Division, is on his way to Washington via the valley.[52] What effect this will have on Grant remains to be seen. Grant has left his lines at Cold Harbor, crossed the Chickahominy with part of his forces at Long Bridge, and gone to Westover, perhaps. Some part of his force appears to have gone to embark at the White House. Lynchburgh is threatened by a portion of Hunter's forces; and a small body of cavalry has crossed the James, and burned the bridge at Concord on the south side of the Railroad. General Lawton, Quartermaster General and his wife, Mrs. Jones, Dr. Richardson and General Elzey spent the evening here and took tea.—Congress adjourned yesterday.—The news of General Polk's being killed by a cannon ball yesterday was in the papers this morning. He was a brave christian soldier, beloved by his troops.—General Ewell is placed in command of Richmond vice Ransom, sent to command the cavalry in the valley. It is a practical *retirement* of the maimed old soldier, to which he must submit on account of his infirmities. He does so sorrowfully and with an ill grace.—Forrest's victory over Grierson at Tishamingo Creek, near Baldwin, is a complete one. He seems to have utterly destroyed the enemy's column, and was still pursuing it relentlessly.

Editor's Notes

1 These were the famous currency reduction and tax bills of February 17, 1864. The first was entitled "An Act to reduce the currency and to authorize a new issue of notes and bonds." The second was entitled "An Act to levy additional taxes for the common defence and support of the Government." See *Statutes at Large of the Confederate States*, Statute IV, Chapter LXIII; and *ibid.*, Chapter LXIV.

2 This was the conscription bill of February 17, 1864. It made all white men between the ages of seventeen and fifty-five liable to military service. It was entitled "An Act to organize forces to serve during the war." See *ibid.*, Statute IV, Chapter LXV.

3 "Mr. Lyon" was probably F. S. Lyon, Representative from Alabama. "Capt. Brown" has not been identified.

4 J. P. Holcombe represented the Confederate States in the legal battle which followed the seizure of the steamship *Chesapeake* off Cape Cod on the morning of December 7, 1863. She was seized by an unauthorized Confederate crew and J. P. Benjamin, Confederate Secretary of State, disclaimed the responsibility of the Confederacy for this act. See J. T. Scharf, *History of the Confederate States Navy*, pp. 812-13.

5 Gorgas refers to the Battle of Olustee, or Ocean Pond, Florida. General Joseph Finnegan's Confederates defeated the Union force under General Truman Seymour in a three-hour fight on the afternoon of February 20, 1864. See *B&L*, IV, 76-80.

6 Julius A. de Lagnel, one of Gorgas's chief assistants.

7 The U.S.S. *Housatonic* was torpedoed and sunk at Charleston on February 17, 1864, by the Confederate submarine *H. L. Hunley.* Gorgas mistook the *H. L. Hunley* for the torpedo boat *David,* probably because the *H. L. Hunley* was fitted out with a spar torpedo in the same manner as the *David,* by order of General Beauregard. See Scharf, *History of the Confederate States Navy,* 760-61; also R. S. Henry, *The Story of the Confederacy,* 340.

8 General William Sooy Smith and Colonel B. H. Grierson. For accounts of this affair, see *OR,* ser. I, vol. 32, pt. 1, 251-62.

9 Probably General G. W. Smith.

10 Grant was made commander of all Union armies on March 9, 1864.

11 R. Milton Cary.

12 Gorgas refers to the Habeas Corpus bill. This was "An Act to suspend the privilege of the writ of habeas corpus in certain cases," passed on February 15, 1864. See *Statutes . . . Confederate States,* Statute IV, Chapter XXXVII.

13 General Henry W. Wessels.

14 General Robert F. Hoke.

15 General Thomas E. G. Ransom, commanding the U. S. XIII Corps under Banks. Ransom was wounded at the Battle of Mansfield, Louisiana, on April 8, 1864. See *B&L,* IV, 354 n.

16 This was the Battle of Mansfield, Louisiana.

17 General Alfred Mouton was killed on April 8, 1864, at Mansfield. See *B&L,* IV, 355 n.

18 Both Generals John M. Jones and Leroy A. Stafford of Lee's Second Corps were killed opposing the Union advance after crossing the Rapidan River at Ely's and Germanna Fords. Lee, in reporting the death of Jones and mortal wounding of Stafford, cited the latter for "conspicuous valor." See *OR,* ser. I, vol. 36, pt. 1, 1028; also Freeman, *Lee's Lieutenants,* III, 513.

19 General William Mahone.

20 Captain E. S. Hutter.

21 General Eppa Hunton.

22 For General Sterling Price's report of operations in Arkansas in March and April, 1864, including various actions with General Frederick Steele's Union forces, see *OR,* ser. I, vol. 34, pt. 1, 779-84.

23 The *Albemarle* had a spirited action on May 5, 1864, with some eight Union ships. She more than held her own, putting two of the enemy out of action. See Scharf, *History of the Confederate States Navy,* pp. 410-12.

24 This movement was carried out and Tallessee Armory became one of the mainstays of the Ordnance Department. See Claude E. Fuller and Richard D. Steuart, *Firearms of the Confederacy*, pp. 150-54. There is a picture of this armory in *ibid.*, facing 152.

25 Truman Seymour and Alexander Shaler. See *B&L*, IV, 127, for circumstances of their capture.

26 This was true. General Albert G. Jenkins engaged Union forces advancing on Dublin, Virginia, on May 9, 1864. Jenkins was defeated and the enemy destroyed the depot at Dublin as well as the New River Bridge. See *B&L*, IV, 477.

27 John McCausland. See *ibid.*, p. 423 for the circumstances of his assumption of command.

28 Archibald Gracie and Seth M. Barton.

29 Harry Hays and James A. Walker.

30 Stuart was mortally wounded at Yellow Tavern on the afternoon of May 11, 1864.

31 Generals Edward Johnson and George H. Steuart.

32 General John Sedgwick was killed near Spotsylvania Court House, Virginia, on May 9, 1864. See *B&L*, IV, 175, for details of his death.

33 Briscoe G. Baldwin.

34 Averell was not captured though he did suffer a check in his advance on Wytheville, Virginia. On May 11, 1864, Morgan repulsed Averell's attack on that town and neighboring lead mines. See *B&L*, IV, 423.

35 General Charles A. Heckman.

36 General John C. Breckinridge and the Virginia Military Institute Cadets defeated General Franz Sigel and his Union forces at New Market, Virginia, on May 15, 1864.

37 General Johnson Hagood.

38 This may have been William R. Lee, colonel of the 20th Massachusetts.

39 This was probably John B. Baldwin, Representative from Virginia. See *Jour. Congress, Confed. States*, vols. 1-7, for his activity in the House.

40 Representative and Mrs. William Porcher Miles of South Carolina. See *ibid.;* and *DAB*, XII, 616-17.

41 John Taylor Wood and J. C. Ives were Aides-de-Camp to the President. See Dunbar Rowland, ed., *Jefferson Davis, Constitutionalist: His Letters, Papers and Speeches*, VI, 232, 416.

42 Andrew Jackson.

43 Philip Kearney.

44 For Beauregard's report of the capture of Walker, see *OR*, ser. I, vol. 36, pt. 3, 820; also *Daily Richmond Examiner*, May 23, 1864, for loss of Walker.

45 Smith Stansbury of Louisiana, was fourth in the class of 1841 at West Point—the class in which Gorgas was sixth. Stansbury was assigned to the ordnance corps, as was Gorgas, but resigned in 1844 to serve as a clerk in a Baltimore banking house from 1848 to 1861. See *Cullum*, II, 65.

46 These were the *Richmond Whig* and *Enquirer*.

47 An account of the incident is in the *Daily Richmond Examiner*, May 28, 1864. The resolution of the House of Representatives read:
"*Resolved*, That the thanks of the House of Representatives of the Confederate States are hereby unanimously tendered to the cadets of the Virginia Military Institute and the officers who command them for their gallant conduct in the battle of the fifteenth instant, near New Market, in the Shenandoah Valley of Virginia.
"*Resolved further*, That the Speaker of the House communicate this resolution to the cadets in such form and at such time as may seem to him proper." See *Jour. Congress, Confed. States*, vol. 7, 90.

48 Colonel Edward Willis was killed while leading General John Pegram's brigade on May 30, 1864. See Freeman, *Lee's Lieutenants*, III, 502.

49 Joseph Mayo.

50 General Jones was killed in an action near Piedmont, Virginia, on June 5, 1864. He was opposing the forces of General David Hunter. See *B&L*, IV, 485-86.

51 Thomas P. Pelot, first lieutenant in the Confederate Navy. He commanded the C. S. privateer *Lady Davis;* the C.S.S. *Savannah* (*Oconee*), *Resolute* and *Georgia*, Savannah Squadron, 1861-64. He was killed on June 3, 1864, while engaged in capturing the *Water Witch*. See *Officers Register, Confederate Navy*, 151.

52 Gorgas means that Early was taking Ewell's Corps northward. Early had assumed command of the Second Corps of the Army of Northern Virginia on May 29, 1864. See Freeman, *Lee's Lieutenants*, III, 498-99.

5 ★ ★ ★

The Spirit Is Willing

June 16th [1864]. Hugh telegraphs that he is better. His brother Gus, and his servant Perry, left last evening and have reached him I hope by this time, 10:00 p.m.—The news from Petersburgh is unfavorable, the enemy having captured a portion of the entrenchments, and some pieces of Sturdivant's battery.[1] I hope General Lee will be able to correct this very soon. It will not do to lose Petersburgh.— A Mr. Austin, an English merchant, spent the evening. Mrs. Commodore Forrest called.[2] They have lost all their wealth and can hardly get their daily bread, it seems. It is sad to see people plunged into utter destitution from a state of entire affluence. Three years ago this lady did not know what it was to want money, or anything that money could buy. Now she is dependent on a portion of her son's pay. He is in the Navy, and gets one hundred dollars a month, and being abroad draws his pay in gold. Of this he gives his mother one-half, worth eight or nine hundred per month.

June 19th. Mary arrived Friday evening. Hugh is improving. She proposes joining him tomorrow. Mrs. Captain Adams is here with us; her husband is also wounded. She is a niece of Dr. Crawford [?].[3]—No fighting at Petersburgh yesterday nor today, a thousand wild rumors to the contrary, one of which was that a great battle had been fought there with the loss of five thousand on ours and 25,000 on the Yankee side! Such rumors prevail mostly on Sundays.

Thursday, June 23rd. Yesterday our right wing attacked the left of the enemy, captured sixteen hundred prisoners, some colors and four guns. The enemy have thrown a few shells into the suburbs of Petersburgh.—Hunter is retreating toward Western Virginia with Early in pursuit. Not much damage has been or is likely to be done to him.—Our forces are inadequate to punish him.—General and Dr. Aiken came today from Hugh. Mary went up with the Doctor on Monday. He is doing well. The wound is close by the jugular vein, and the ball came out eight inches down by the back bone, Hugh having been in a stooping posture when shot. Colonel Mallet,[4] who has been staying with us a few days, left us this evening. I am taking daily rides hoping to restore my strength which is somewhat shaken.

June 24th. The news from Petersburg is still good. The party which occupied the Weldon Railroad, below P., was driven off and five hundred prisoners captured. The enemy took possession of Burkeville last night, but have been dislodged after doing some damage. They took, it is said, the direction of the high bridge on the south side road. Willie and I saw the prisoners marched thro' town this morning —a dirty set.

June 26th. The enemy have cut the Danville Road in various placés, and tho' they have been driven from the Weldon Road below Petersburgh, their proximity to that Road renders it practically valueless to us. We are thus for the present without communication with the South. Fortunately we are provided with meat for forty days, and with the wheat which we shall soon get from Central Virginia, many will laugh at Grant's efforts at a "seige" as he terms it.—Hampton attacked the enemy's cavalry (Sheridan) near Charles City C. H. yesterday and drove it from its position with loss. General Lee speaks of it as a very handsome affair. Our loss in the attack by Hagood on Friday (probably a reconnaisance) on the City Point Road is stated by General Lee at 93 killed and wounded, and 207

[?] missing.—Hunter appears to have disappeared into Western Virginia, with some loss of artillery and wagons. The Yankees now systematically shoot their worn down horses. Can anything be more diabolical than thus to treat their noble animals?—This is the hottest day we have yet had.

June 30th. No striking military events have occurred, if we except that Johnston telegraphs he repulsed a general attack of the enemy with "supposed" heavy loss. There are no particulars and I have little confidence in the state of affairs in that quarter. I fully expect to hear of his retreat behind Atlanta, probably in the direction of West Point.— Early is at Staunton and down the valley, his artillery having been heard of at Port Republic. I hope another invasion of Maryland is not contemplated, yet there is no other explanation of this movement. The raiders have left the line of the Danville Railroad and made their way back to Grant's main body. They were decidedly repulsed at the Staunton River bridge by the "Reserve" forces stationed there. Our friends the two Aikens and Colonel Mallet left yesterday by way of Petersburgh for the South.—Gold has certainly risen to 244 and some say is selling at 5 premium in Washington, (five dollars in "greenbacks" for one in gold).

July 1st. 15 minutes a.m. It is after midnight and Minnie and I are sitting up waiting for Hugh and Mary who started from Louisa C. H. on the Central Road. Something has doubtless delayed the train which was due at 6:00 p.m. There is good news from below Petersburgh, where the returning raiders were attacked and defeated with heavy loss of prisoners, horses, and wagons. It is surmised that Grant is preparing a grand bombardment of Petersburgh for the 4th of July.—Mr. Memminger, Secretary of Treasury, resigned his post a few days ago, but continues on duty until his successor is appointed. No name is yet mentioned. The President sent for me day before yesterday to show me a big sword made at Columbia, S. C., and sent to him. He seemed to think highly of it, tho' I objected to its length. He opened the conversation by saying as he took the sword to hand it to me: "Colonel, I find my conversations with you have more reason and less politics than any others." He likes to talk of matters purely military, especially about guns etc., which he used to pay much attention to as Secretary of War under Mr. Pierce.—A little girl was born to him day before yesterday.

I am 46 years old today. I may still live to see the country recover from the effects of this terrible war, if it should come soon.

July 3rd. The number of prisoners taken below Petersburgh is ascertained thus far at about one thousand, and seven hundred darkeys recaptured. The Yankee cavalry seems dispersed over the country in bad plight, giving itself up in squads. Little mercy is shown to them by our cavalry —they are shot down wherever found. A Confederate Naval officer, coming from Wilmington to Richmond, was surrounded by them, and seeing his shoulder straps, drew their revolvers shouting: "Kill him, kill him!—no prisoners," and but for the negro boys with him they would have fired upon him. Our people are exasperated to the last degree by the burning, plundering and maltreatment inflicted by these marauding scoundrels.—Tomorrow (4th) will be Grant's great day, and if he does nothing he will inflict great disappointment on his admirers. Only one or two houses have thus far been burned in Petersburgh. The Danville Railroad has been destroyed for about 28 miles beyond Burkeville, and it will take three weeks to repair it, say until the 20th of July. In the meantime we have very little corn to live on. Wagon trains will no doubt be established at the break.—Hugh arrived last evening, in pretty good condition.

July 7th. No fighting at Petersburgh. It is reported that Early met Pope and Sigel at Martinsburg, and captured 1200 prisoners. Would that we could hear of no more captures. The war has now assumed that phase in which no mercy can be shown to the enemy. He burns, robs, murders and ravishes, and this is to be met only by killing all. Johnston has, I fear, fallen behind the Chattahoochie, just as I surmised long ago. Will he fight at last? I do not expect it, and yet I do not see how he *can* give up Atlanta without a fight—a general action. An expedition is it seems in preparation at Wilmington, looking to the liberation of the prisoners at Point Lookout. I know nothing of it, except what I hear, but was directed to send two thousand stand of arms there at once. It seems, however, impossible to keep State Secrets, and the expedition is talked of in the streets. —We had just a sprinkling of rain today after five weeks of total drought. There was scarce enough to lay the dust. Hugh is evidently getting stronger daily.—The resignation of Chase, the Yankee Secretary of Treasury, and the rise of gold to over 250 are the chief subjects of interest in the Northern papers.

July 10th. Sunday. The drought still continues and the weather is very warm. Tonight there is a strong breeze from the South which may eventually blow up a rain.— Bad news from beyond the sea. The "Alabama" was sunk by the "Kearsarge" after a combat of one hour and forty minutes, on the 19th of June. Captain Semmes and most of the officers and crew were picked up by an English yacht, the "Grayhound," which carried them to Southampton. The fight took place off Cherbourg.—News from the North of the 6th and 7th places gold at 259. The new Yankee Secretary of Treasury, Fessenden, had been installed.—The progress of Early created some alarm, and troops for one hundred days were called out in Pennsylvania, New York and Massachusetts. He was in possession of the Baltimore and Ohio Railroad from a few miles east of Cumberland to below Harper's Ferry, and had captured a good deal of property and stores.—At Charleston the Yankees made an attack on James Island (Fort Johnson) on the 3rd of July and were repulsed with the loss of five

to six hundred killed, wounded and captured.—From Mobile
General Maury telegraphs that he is threatened with an
attack. The enemy appears to have advanced upon Jackson
from Vicksburgh and to have occupied it, but at last accounts were retiring upon their lines.—At Petersburgh the
enemy is using mortars with effect upon the city, and
burning a good many houses. A few days ago a party landed
at the fine plantation of Curls Neck and destroyed by fire
the entire crop of wheat in the fields.

July 13th. It is reported that General Lee has gone to
Georgia,—General Bragg has certainly gone. Everybody
has at last come to the conclusion that Johnston has retreated far enough. Mr. Hill is, I understand, here on the
mission of getting additional troops (cavalry) to operate
on the communications of General Sherman, as the only
means of saving Atlanta—and what is to be done must be
done quickly, they say. He wants the forces of General S. D.
Lee (Lt. General) bro't over from Mississippi for this purpose.—The news from the North to the 9th shows great
excitement over the appearance of Early's columns on the
Potomac. They are unable to decide whether there are five
thousand or thirty-five thousand men there. Our forces
seem to have advanced into the skirts of Pennsylvania.—
Nothing farther heard of the column reported by Maury as
marching upon Mobile from New Orleans. The enemy do
not appear to make any impression on Charleston or its
defences.—An expedition to liberate the prisoners at Point
Lookout has been on foot at Wilmington for some time
past. The removal of the prisoners to Elmira, New York,
renders that prospect abortive. Early movements alarmed
the enemy at this point.—It rained briskly several hours
day before yesterday but the earth was so baked that it
appears to have done little good.—The death of poor Captain Walter Wynne, at Petersburgh, of a wound in the knee,
reached us last evening. Amelia knew him as a boy, and
his sisters. It is a sad thing. His wife is on the way here
but had not arrived at the date of his death.

July 14th. News to the 11th from the North announces
the defeat of their own forces at Monocacy on the 9th, with
the capture of General Tyler and Colonel Seward.[5] Our
troops seem to be moving toward Baltimore. It is still unknown here whether or no General Lee has gone to Atlanta.
I presume he has not, as such a thing could hardly be kept
secret, he being too well known personally along the line of
railroads.—In Mississippi our forces on the 11th were at
Pontotoc, while the enemy was at New Albany and moving
forward slowly. A battle has probably occurred of which
we shall hear soon.—At Charleston, various attacks of the
enemy on John's and James Island have been repulsed.

The weather continues warm and the drought destroys
our gardens, the rains of Monday having been of no great
extent. Partial rains are, however, occurring about us which
will keep the corn from burning up.

Major Walker,[6] General Randolph, Mr. I. Alfred Jones
and Bayne dined with us yesterday.

July 17th. Early defeated the enemy at Monocacy and
then appears to have advanced upon Washington, whether
with a view to make a dash upon it or simply to frighten
it is not known. He has, however, again withdrawn, and on
Tuesday last was on the retreat. Doubtless he is by this
time behind the Potomac. The only good he has done is to
arouse the waning enthusiasm at the North and draw a few
additional recruits to their standard. He will lose a good
many struggles [stragglers?] on his way back to the val-.
ley.—S. D. Lee seems to have attacked the enemy in position at Tupelo, and been repulsed. He says it was a *drawn
fight.*

Took a long ride last evening out by the Brooke Road
to the intermediate lines, along those to Grove Road, and
back by that about twelve or thirteen miles. Major Pierson,
from Europe, and Colonel McLean,[7] Quartermaster's Department, spent the evening. Major P. is a Frenchman in
our service, who has served bravely for some time in the
Artillery. He has been at home.—The drought still con-

tinues, the little rain a week ago having done no perceptible good.

July 19th. Johnston has been relieved of his command and Hood placed in charge of the Army. This, of course, means fighting, and a battle must soon be the result. General J. will doubtless have a strong party who will condemn his removal.—Rumors have been rife for several days that Grant is dead, believed by many but hardly true. —A slow rain has done a great deal of good, and the clouds look as if it might continue.

July 22nd. A fight took place day before yesterday on the Chattahoochie, in which we were the assailants, and as the despatch says, "drove the enemy to their breastworks." An attack was made on Wheeler's Cavalry and repulsed.—A despatch I received from Columbus says that place is threatened by a heavy force and the Ordnance Stores and machinery were being sent away from there. So, after having run to Columbus from Baton Rouge, we have run from Columbus to some other place. Too much running, and too little fighting, General Joe Johnston.

P. M. A despatch from General Hood announces an attack on General Cleburne's Division of Hardee's corps, and on Wheeler's Cavalry on the right, and that the attack was handsomely repulsed. Colonel Adams, 33rd Alabama, killed. In the previous attack General Stevens (of Charleston) was mortally wounded.—People are, I think, generally satisfied with the removal of General Johnston. They have praised him, and waited for him to fight until he has lost all of Georgia, and they have gotten tired of him. Nevertheless if Hood fights and is victorious there will be plenty who will exclaim: "behold the fruits of Johnston's strategy," while if he is defeated these people will cry: "see the fruits of the removal of Johnston!" The Administration will gain nothing in the estimation of such in either case. It is a pity President Davis did not act earlier on his own judgment, which has been adverse to Johnston. His tardy action was at last induced by the action of distinguished Georgians represented by Senator Hill,[8] who came on here after a full interview with General Johnston, and urged a change of commanders, having ascertained to his entire satisfaction that Johnston would not fight even for Atlanta, but would continue to retrograde under the flanking movements of Sherman.

July 23rd. A despatch from General Hood states that the enemy attacked yesterday and were repulsed after which our troops assumed the offensive. General Hardee on the right moved around the enemy's left to his rear, capturing fifteen hundred prisoners and sixteen guns. General Cheatham, in the centre, captured five hundred prisoners and six guns; five stands of colors also captured. General Wheeler drove the enemy's cavalry back at Decatur. We have lost Major General W. H. T. Walker, killed and Brig-General Smith [?], Gist and Merch* [Mercer] wounded.[9] Our loss, I fear, is heavy. The success appears to have been decided. Hardee is represented in a former despatch as being still upon the enemy's flanks and rear. McPherson is reported killed, by Yankee prisoners.—At Petersburgh the enemy is reported moving across the Appomattox; and our "local" forces are ordered to hold themselves in readiness.—News from the North places gold at 263, and the tone of the papers is desponding.—In the valley our forces are said to have defeated the enemy at Snicker's Gap, and to have driven him across the Shenandoah, we holding Winchester.—On the whole the atmosphere brightens, but we cannot predict what a day may bring forth.

July 26th. The "situation" here appears to be unchanged, except that the enemy have thrown some troops to the north bank of the River, at Deep Bottom. A Yankee regiment was run over by our troops yesterday and utterly broken up, but we only succeeded in securing 48 prisoners.—Heavy

*Error of despatches.

firing of artillery continues at Petersburgh, with great waste of ammunition, no doubt unavoidable.—From Atlanta Hood corrects his first despatch and now reports thirteen in place of 22 guns and 18 stands of colors in place of five. General Mercer not wounded. The enemy is now throwing occasional shells into Atlanta, and appears to have gotten to the Railroad at Stone Mountain. He has also broken up say twenty miles of the West Point and M. Railroad, and is at Opelika. This party, it is said, is directing its course toward Andersonville to release the prisoners there, (now 30,000). There is a dispatch tonight from General Lee saying that Early had attacked Crook[10] at Kernstown and routed him driving him beyond Winchester.—The community is a good deal stirred up at the publication from Yankee sources of the correspondence between Messrs Holcombe, Clay and George Saunders on the one side, and Greely and Lincoln on the other, relative to peace. It is not flattering to us.[11]

July 28th. A disgraceful affair occurred yesterday morning at seven o'clock, below Chaffin's Farm. The Yankees attacked a battery of 20-pounder Parrott guns and captured it, our supports flying without firing a gun —and yet these supports were Kershaw's[12] own brigade— some of the best in the service. They were *flanked*, it seems, on their left and at once ran, leaving the battery (Rockbridge's Artillery) to its fate. The Captain fired, he told me, double canister, and at last saved his caissons and limbers with all the horses. The President sent for me yesterday to ask me something about the number of men that could be spared to go out to the trenches without suspending work. He read me an extract from a letter written by a high French military authority calling attention to the use of rockets, against shipping and cavalry. He is looking quite well, but is growing not only gray but white with his cares.

July 28th. The enemy appears to have crossed to the north side of the James in force and to threaten us from there. The local forces were called out today, it being reported that cavalry had moved toward our left, and might threaten the city from the north east. It appears probable that we shall soon hear of forces from the Trans-Mississippi having crossed over into Tennessee to operate on Sherman's communications there. Little Rock is undoubtedly now in our possession and Arkansas is redeemed.—Spent the evening at Major Ellicott's,[13] who has a charming wife, and who gave a pleasant supper, (tea or coffee). Dr. McCaw and wife there.—This morning Dr. Spotswood, Mr. Aubrey,[14] Colonel Aiken and Bayne breakfasted with us—a very nice breakfast of one chicken and tomato omelette! The weather is quite warm but the breeze good. We need rain again.

July 31st, Sunday. Grant, it appears, sprung a mine under one of our batteries at Petersburgh yesterday, and did some damage, but failed to break our lines. The enemy were, it seems, recrossing to the south side and we were yesterday following the movement. — A fight of some severity appears to have been going on at Atlanta on the 27th, as it is reported from Macon on the 28th, yet we have no definite or official news concerning it. Stewart and Wheeler were both said to be wounded.—Went to Drury's Bluff yesterday to see the examination of the midshipmen on the "Patrick Henry" (Yorktown). There were about thirty. The examination was very cursory in navigation, firing, making sail and broadsword exercise. The little "Squib" torpedo boat passed us. She is only about 45 feet long, and makes about nine miles. This is the little boat used against the "Minnesota." Others of the same sort are building. Lt. Parker[15] commands the "Patrick Henry"— Mr. Hall[16] is her first officer.

P. M. Good news from Petersburgh. In repelling the attack of the enemy after firing their mine, an assault appears to have ensued, which resulted in the capture of 850 privates and 75 commissioned officers, including General Bartlett[17]

and his Staff—twelve stands of colors and the recapture
of the guns which had been taken with the position. Five
hundred dead Yankees were left on the spot. General
Mahone's division appears to have done the work. The
enemy seem to have returned chiefly to the south side.
Grant is certainly at his wit's end, and is simply moving
his men about idly and without plan.—No good news yet
from Georgia.

August 3rd. The news from Georgia yesterday was
cheering. Stoneman with five hundred of his raiding cavalry were captured by General Iverson, not far from Macon
and bro't into that city.[18] They were first repulsed from
Macon by the "Reserves" and in retreating were attacked
and routed by General Iverson. The remainder of the command (originally 2800) were dispersed thro' the country.
So that party has, as the saying is "come to grief." In an
attack on the 27th on our left Stewart and Loring were
wounded, and the day before General Rector. Our losses
have been quite heavy, as I see the enemy reports the arrival of over a thousand prisoners at Louisville, in the
operations of the 19th to the 22nd of July.—A bad accident
occurred in the Armory close by yesterday. An armorer
(Smoot) drawing one of the guns to be repaired toward
him it exploded and the ball passed thro' the ankle joint.
In two hours afterward his leg was cut off some distance
above the joint. He is lying in the office at the other end
of this building and Mamma looks after him occasionally
and sends him his meals. It is a sad affair to this poor
working man. His wife is some distance in the country.

August 6th. Nothing new of special interest.—The burning of Chambersburgh by Early gives intense satisfaction.
General McCausland seems to have been in command of
the troops who did the deed,—a very good one.—It is stated
in the papers this morning that the officers recently placed
under fire in Charleston, and at Morris Island, have been

exchanged—a good solution of our awkward move.—General Johnston is said to be in town, for what purpose is not known.

August 7th. The news of the destruction of our fleet at Mobile creates no surprise; nothing but disaster comes from that unfortunate branch of the service. The news, which is meagre, represents that we have lost three ironclads—one captured by the enemy (the "Tennessee"), one sunk and one blown up.[19] What effect this will have toward the capture of Mobile remains to be seen—not much I think—tho' I fear it will lead to the reduction of Forts Morgan and Gaines.—Beauregard, it seems, sprung a mine yesterday (or evening before) under some works of the enemy, blowing up their mines, and doing some damage. I hope it may be so, but I haven't much faith in the report. Troops were moving from Petersburgh thro' town yesterday—destination unknown.

August 8th. Admiral Buchanan[20] has, it seems, lost a leg and been captured. The "Tennessee' and "Selma" are captured; the "Gaines" is ashore and the "Morgan" alone escaped. The first is alone ironclad. The whole of Longstreet's command and Fitz Lee's cavalry are said to have moved northward. I doubt whether more than a Division and the Cavalry have yet gone. It is probable that Grant too is sending off troops.—The northern papers, it is said, announce the removal of Meade and the appointment of Hooker, on account of the disaster of Saturday, (the mine).—The drought still continues to the total destruction, I fear, of all crops, especially of our vegetables.—I omitted to note heretofore the accession to our domestic establishment of a good milch cow. She was taken out of her stables at Petersburgh "under fire." She adds greatly to the good living of the children, and of us all.

August 10th. The news from Mobile continues decidedly bad. Fort Gaines appears to have been shamefully surrendered by its commander, Lieutenant-Colonel Chas. Anderson, with its garrison of six hundred men. It could have held out for three months, and was provisioned for six. This is indeed shameful.—There are rumors of the capture of a considerable portion of Bradley Johnson and McCausland's commands.—A portion of the fifty exchanged officers from Charleston arrived a few days ago. These officers were the ones sent by the enemy to be placed on Morris Island as retaliation for placing fifty of theirs in Charleston. For a weak measure it has turned out very well. Mary is quite ailing and we begin to feel anxious about her condition. Hugh's wound is nearly well, but he is far from strong. No rain yet. Willie and I took a bath in the river last evening.

August 12th. The Yankees claim that they surprised and captured a portion of McCausland's and Bradley Johnson's command at Romney, with wagons and artillery. Some such thing happened, I fear, but not to the extent named.—The explosion which was lately heard in the Yankee lines at Petersburgh seems to have been an explosion of powder and shells at City Point—a great many employees killed and wounded.—An Artillery officer just from Atlanta gives me a gloomy view of the situation. The probability is that the city must be evacuated, as the enemy is closing his lines about it. They extend from the river to near the Macon Railroad. That once seriously endangered the city, must, of course, be evacuated.—There are no intelligible explanations of the surrender of Fort Gaines. Colonel Anderson was, it appears, two years at West Point. Saw yesterday one of the exchanged officers, General Archer,[21] but had no opportunity to talk with him.

August 14th. The President sent for me yesterday to tell me about a report that the powder at Battery Danzler (Howlett's Farm) had given very inferior ranges. He was reading to Mr. Mallory and Mr. Seddon a report from General Lee that the Yankees were at work digging a canal across Dutch Gap; and told Mr. Mallory with his usual

clearness what would be the effect of the "cut-off" then
made, viz: that the depth of water above will be diminished
while below it will be increased. This he illustrated by cit-
ing instances of similar effects on the Mississippi, and referred to General Bragg in proof of one where lands were
reclaimed above the "cut-off." Having stated the general
effect, he called Mr. Mallory's attention to the position of
his ironclads—asked him at what point above the Dutch
Gap was the first bar, and whether his ironclads might
not be caught below it, unable to return; adding after discussing the matter: "very well Mr. Mallory, forward is
forward." He then went on to discuss what could be done
to interfere with the cutting of the canal.—Talking to me
of an officer, (Colonel L. M. Clarke of Mo.) who was at
West Point with him, he said: "He is a good, conscientious
man, with abilities of various sort. He can draw, and has
a fondness for machinery. He is out of position—has lost
two sons—one at school, having been killed by a Dutch boy
on account of his politics; the other in command of a battery in one of the battles in Missouri. He has been sick and
has had something like paralysis. He has now nothing to
do tho' willing to do anything. I dislike to see such a man
walking about trying to get into position, looking like a
horse outside the lot at fodder time!" He then asked me
whether I could do anything with him, and seemed relieved
when I told him that I had appropriate duty. He spoke
again of a long sabre that General Hampton wanted made
for his cavalry, and remembered that on a previous occasion
he spoke of the armament of cavalry, and said that if they
had sabres they should not have guns, but be made to depend on the sabre. He referred to the "pistol carbine," the
barrel of which was twelve inches long, and had a movable
stock, which he had adopted in the United States service
when Secretary of War. He referred to it as "the old government," which somewhat attracted my attention. He tho't
that if our cavalry were to depend on the sabre alone that

they would then come to close quarters, and run off their antagonists who depend on their long range guns.

No news and no rain.

August 17th. A sharp engagement took place yesterday on the Charles City road below White's Tavern, in which the enemy were driven back. We lost General Girardey killed, and General Chambliss[22] wounded and, it is believed, a prisoner. No details of our other losses seem to be known. It seems to have been a tolerably determined attempt of the enemy to break thro' our lines on the north side of James River.—The day before we lost four 8-inch howitzers which were in position to shell the enemy's pontoon bridge at Deep Bottom. The infantry supports appear to have been again at fault. These guns were in charge of Lieutenant Colonel Pemberton.[23] General G.[24] was advanced from the grade of Captain A.A.G. to that of Brigadier, and commanded Wright's G. Brigade.—Our local forces were again called out yesterday in consequence of the proximity of the enemy. They go with reluctance, and only one-fourth were present last evening for the "march."—From Georgia there is nothing cheering. It is probable that Atlanta will be given up, and East Point held.—A heavy force of the enemy under A. J. Smith appears to be advancing thro' north Mississippi. Forrest has but seven thousand men to hold them in check. He was last at Oxford. A division of the Trans-Mississippi Army was to cross the River tomorrow; its strength not over five thousand. We ought to have twelve or fifteen thousand men to operate on Sherman's communications in middle Tennessee.—Wheeler left Atlanta on the 10th to cut Sherman's communications—not yet heard from.—The enemy appear to have come up pretty close to Mobile, but the city will be held at all hazards.—A good rain on Monday and cloudy and showery since.

Sunday, August 21st. General Hill attacked Warren's[25] (5th) Corps on the Railroad south of Petersburgh, and captured 24 to 2700 prisoners, among them General Hayes[26] and some sixty commissioned officers—this on Friday. On Saturday the attack was attempted to be renewed, but it was found that the enemy had massed their two Army Corps, and the attack was deferred. It is reported that a heavy fight has been going on today.—A despatch received from General Lee today states that Early attacked the enemy at Front Royal and captured two hundred prisoners, the enemy retreating toward Harper's Ferry, burning the wheat in stacks and in the fields. A heavy force of the enemy appears to be advancing in Mississippi, and Governor Clarke is assembling the Reserves. Urgent calls for arms there, which the break in the W. Pt. and Montgomery Railroad renders it difficult to get forward. The "Tallahassee," Captain J. T. Wood,[27] is doing excellent service capturing and burning the shipping of the enemy on the coast, as far up as New England.—News from Northern papers show that Wheeler is operating on Sherman's communications at Dalton, breaking the Railroad and destroying supply trains.

August 24th. The attack on the enemy's position upon the Weldon Road, on Sunday, was a decided failure. Our troops were not up, the crossing back from this side not having been effected until Monday morning. The enemy is now firmly established on and across the Weldon Road, his left extending to over a mile to the west of it. This is a serious advantage gained by him. Our loss was not very heavy and chiefly in Hagood's brigade. This from being one of the largest brigades, when it came from South Carolina here about the 1st of May, is now reduced to not many hundreds. No news of interest from Mobile, since the surrender of Fort Gaines.—The Yankee papers report that Farragut had ordered an attack on Fort Morgan on a certain morning, but it did not appear to have been made. They say that General Granger[28] has invested Fort M. on the land side. This is not reported from Mobile. In the Valley nothing has been heard of Sheridan since his retreat down the Valley before Early. The cavalry there is very inferior and should be thoroughly re-organized.—From the Mississippi we hear that Dick Taylor has suspended the movement to this side of the River in consequence of the desertions from his ranks. His troops will not serve on this side if they can help it. If we get no troops from Trans-Mississippi the plan of operations for the relief of Hood will be seriously interfered with.—A flag of truce on Monday bore, I hope, to the North the papers necessary for the exchange of Dick, so that he *may* be among us in a short time.—The yellow fever is making havoc at Bermuda. Several of our clerks have died there and others are down with the fever.

August 26th. No news of special importance. Rumors of fighting at Petersburgh yesterday.—Gayle[29] is still very ill, and parents much distressed.

August 29th. Midnight. I have just returned from the sick bed of poor little Gayle. He is struggling hard to hold on to the little remnant of life still left to him. If a mother's love and devotion can get him thro' he will live. She still has hope, despite the doctor's sad conviction that he will die. His disease seems to be in the chest, and is manifested by hot fever, great debility and attenuation, and chiefly by violent paroxysms of pain, which at first made him writhe, but appear to be diminishing in violence. Whether this is a symptom of amendment or decline remains to be seen.—The fight on Thursday was severe and resulted in the capture of over two thousand prisoners and nine cannon, with several stands of colors by Hill's Corps and Hampton's Cavalry. The enemy were dislodged from their works towards Reams' Station tho' still holding on to their position alongside of and east of the Railroad. It has cost them ten thousand men thus far *captured* and perhaps half that number in killed and wounded. Can we hold out much longer? The captured, killed and wounded, tho' half that of the enemy are still seriously depleting us. I doubt whether

Lee now has thirty thousand men of all arms under his and Beauregard's joint command.—Hood says the enemy is contracting his lines, and is now nowhere nearer than four miles from Atlanta. It is supposed that he has had to send off a portion of his force to recover his communications, interrupted by Wheeler.—The surrender of Fort Morgan seems certain. The circumstances are not yet known. All that Mobile business indicates a poor head, Maury.—The "Tallahassee" is safe back in Wilmington after her destructive cruise. Another vessel, the "Edith," is nearly ready to go out on a like errand of vengeance against the enemy's commerce. Peace begins to be very openly talked about.—I saw the President last week on the subject of the promotion or appointment of some officers. He talked about various subjects. Showed me a telegram from Hood, saying that a brigade of infantry and cavalry had driven off a party of raiders and captured colors and a gun. "He says nothing of prisoners," remarked the President, significantly, and repeated the remark so that I could not misunderstand what he meant—that Hood did not choose to take prisoners when the enemy went on such errands—and such is the sentiment of the country. He was inclined to be dissatisfied at the loss of the "Tennessee" without being injured. A letter from one of her officers explains that her wheel and afterward her rudder tackle were shot away, and she lay unmanageable. The 15-inch shot penetrated the iron but did no great damage, not coming quite thro'.—In the attack on Friday, week, General Saunders[30] was killed. He was from Alabama and the youngest Brigadier yet made, being only 24 years old.

August 31st. Hood telegraphs that the enemy has wholly changed his position, his left being thrown back to the Chattahoochie, and his right resting at some point near the West Pt. Railroad beyond East Point. This takes him beyond shelling distance from Atlanta.—I saw General Hoke today who tells me that they have ceased to fear Grant, and believe themselves to be his equal in numbers.

Our lines are so strong that no assault can be made on them with success. Our ranks are again filling by men returning to duty. Hoke was made a Major General for the capture of Plymouth, but has not maintained his reputation. He is a very pleasant looking young man of rather sanguine disposition, I judge.—Gayle is, I fear, declining, and there is little hope of his getting better.

September 2nd. No news of importance from the points of chief interest. I judge from the length of a telegram from General S. Jones that he apprehends an attack on Charleston by the fleet, as he calls for large supplies of rifle projectiles.—Gayle is still alive but hopes of his recovery are very feeble.—The weather for the last three days has been quite cool.

September 4th. General Hood telegraphs that he has evacuated Atlanta, and is now some twenty or twenty-five miles south on the Macon Road, at Lovejoy's Station. The series of events which led to this seem to have been that Hardee's Corps and Lee's were sent to Jonesboro to counteract a movement of the enemy by his right flank. That these two corps made a feeble attack on the enemy, who had effected a lodgment on the east of the Flint River, and were unsuccessful; that Lee was withdrawn and in his absence the whole weight of the enemy was thrown at his single corps, and he was driven back with the loss of eight pieces of artillery. To prevent the isolation and destruction of this corps Hood had to leave Atlanta and effect a junction with it which he has done, with what loss of stores does not yet appear. This is disastrous, tho' the mere acquisition of Atlanta by the enemy cannot be of much value to him now. Hardee is said to have inflicted heavy loss on the enemy in the engagement. Efforts must now be made to cover Augusta, and for this perhaps all the local and reserve forces there have been sent to the front.—Gayle appears to be better, and strong hopes are entertained of his improvement. He appears again to be conscious.—No movements about Petersburgh. General Lee was in town today.

Wednesday, Sept. 7th. Gayle died this morning at 4:00 o'clock. He began to sink rapidly yesterday morning. The funeral service takes place at 5:30 p.m., today, and the body is taken to Mobile by Mr. Bayne and a friend, Mr. Chalaron. —Hood telegraphs that the enemy is retiring from his front in the direction of Jonesboro. It is quite apparent that Hood besides being out-numbered is out-generaled; yet the enemy have gained no great advantage. The Northern papers announce that McClellan and Pendleton (of Ohio) are the nominees of the Democratic Convention at Chicago. Pendleton is a decided peace man, but with such successes as Mobile and Atlanta there will be little left for the peace party to stand on, as the Republicans think.

September 9th. The enemy are retiring from their advanced position at Jonesboro upon Atlanta, preparatory to another campaign. It is confidentially whispered that Hood has applied to have Hardee relieved, and that General Dick Taylor be assigned in his place. It is also rumored that Beauregard is to be assigned to the command of the Army at Atlanta—not at all probable. It would, however, be popular. The general judgment is that Hood has not capacity for such a command. The President is strongly prejudiced against Beauregard.—No news from Early.—Grant is said to be building a railroad from City Point to the left of his line on the Weldon Railroad.

September 12th. We lost at Atlanta one hundred cars and six engines—an Ordnance train of ammunition and large supplies of Commissary Stores. These latter were distributed to the people.—Sherman has directed all the white inhabitants to be removed from Atlanta—those taking the Oath North, the rest South.—Hood has consented to an armistice for ten days for this purpose.

General Jno. H. Morgan was surprised and killed on Sunday morning (4th Sept.) at the house of Mrs. Williams, in Greenville, East Tennessee. He, with his Staff, slept there and were betrayed to the enemy at Bull's Gap by her daughter, who rode thither, informed of his whereabouts and returned with the enemy. He was killed fighting, endeavoring to escape. The rest were captured. He was determined not to be taken. He was buried with military honors at Abingdon on Monday evening at sunset. It is singular that with his habits and vigilance he should have slept at a house so far advanced without the amplest precautions against surprise.

September 15th. No especial news. I saw General Lee today looking very well. He returned to Petersburgh today. Met today Governor Lubbock of Texas, who has been made A.D.C. to the President. He is a small, middle-aged man, with pleasant open face.

What a farce it is to have here "Senators" from Kentucky—especially such Senators as Sims[31]—a long, lank, unprepossessing man, who they say is making money here in speculations.—I go to Danville in the morning.

September 24th. I returned from Danville Tuesday, 20th, having passed three days there very pleasantly. It is a not unattractive town of about four thousand inhabitants.

On the 17th General Wade Hampton penetrated to the rear of Grant's Army at Sycamore Church and captured 2450 beef cattle and near three hundred prisoners with some wagons, arms etc. About the same day Early was attacked by Sheridan in front of Winchester and defeated with heavy loss on both sides. Generals Rodes and Godwin[32] killed and Fitz Lee and York, (La.), wounded. Our troops fought well but were overpowered. I fear our so-called cavalry, in the Valley, behaved badly. Early fell back to a position in front of Strasburg, said to be very strong, but it was reported yesterday that he had been again worsted and driven back. The reports from Georgia represent the people as very despondent and ready to make terms with the enemy. It is even currently reported that Stephens, Toombs and Brown have had a conference with Sherman. This is of course an exaggeration, but it is *believed* and shows the state of the country. The President went south on Tuesday.—I learned yesterday that our Navy prisoners would be exchanged, and we may expect Dick in the course of a month.

September 25th. Early was again attacked in his position at Fisher's Hill and defeated, retiring with the loss of twelve pieces of artillery and a *few men* to New Market. These recurring defeats are due, it is said, to the inferior quality of our cavalry, which is routed by the enemy's cavalry, who then gets into our rear. Hood is at Lagrange edging off toward Sherman's communications which will force him to fight probably out of Atlanta. If he should beat him in such an encounter Sherman and all his stores would be ours. God grant it! We need a victory to close this bloody year. It is believed, and hoped, that Beauregard will take command of Hood's army. There is little doubt that Grant, who has again returned to his forces, will now soon move. With the disasters in the Valley Lee must meet him with greatly diminished forces. I doubt whether he can now bring thirty thousand infantry into line. The time is coming now when it will be necessary to put our Slaves into the field and let them fight *for their freedom*, in other words give up a part of *the institution* to save the country, *or the whole* if necessary to win independence.

September 27th. Early is still retreating tho' it is *rumored* that he has checked the enemy near Port Republic. These reverses in the Valley will greatly augment our difficulties in holding Richmond this Fall campaign, now about to begin.—Longstreet has doubtless assumed command by this time.—In the South Hardee has been relieved of the command of his Corps at his own request.—President Davis was in Macon on Friday last.—Rode along the fortifications of the "intermediate line" from the James River above the city to the Mechanicsville turnpike about ten miles, making a ride of about twenty miles. The line is continuous with places for artillery at the various roads leading to the city, and at other commanding positions.

The news from Forrest is that he has captured Athens, Ala., with 1300 prisoners, five hundred horses, fifty wagons, arms, etc. It is to be hoped that the tide of reverses has ebbed and that we may hope for victories again. All will, however, depend on what we can do against Grant who must soon move now.

September 29th. The enemy's cavalry is reported to be on a raid thro' the upper portions of the valley. The depot, iron bridge, etc., at Waynesboro, are reported destroyed. Early appears to hold the infantry and artillery of Sheridan in check near Port Republic.—Gold at the North has fallen to 199—indication of very exuberant confidence on their part. It is a curious nation. Why should they exult over a little victory like that at Winchester and at Fisher's Hill? They have lost almost all they held in the Trans-Miss., and have gained nothing in Virginia during this campaign. What they have gained in Georgia they have lost in Mississippi, North Alabama and North Carolina. They think these little reverses are evidences of exhausted resources, but really we are better off now than we were two years ago when no one doubted our ability to wage the War. The only point against us is the scarcity of men to fill up our Armies. This must be met by placing negroes in ranks, giving them their freedom. We must meet the use the North makes of our negroes by using them ourselves, and giving them the same reward.

September 30th. Yesterday and today have again been days of excitement. The whole population of the city has been turned out and armed and sent to the defences. In the morning yesterday the enemy attacked and carried Fort Harrison, one of the outworks of Chaffin's Farm. But few were in the Fort, and it was easily taken by the enemy. Lt. Col. Maury,[33] commanding Chaffin's Bluff, and Major —— an artillery officer, have not been heard of since and were doubtless captured. Soon after an assault was made on

Fort Gilman, another dependency which was repelled decisively. The assault was made in part by negro troops and their loss was heavy, tho' some of them actually clambered out of the deep ditch of the work, up the slope and got into the work. About two hundred of the enemy were killed, and four or five hundred captured.—Today there has been an effort to re-capture Fort Harrison. The first attempt, feebly made, failed—the result of the second has not yet been learned. Our loss has not yet been heavy.

October 2nd. Sunday. The weather was very bad yesterday, and there is little improvement today. We did not retake Fort Harrison, and the attempt is given up. Retrenchments are to be made which will exclude Fort Harrison and give us a good line. During the operations on this flank the enemy advanced on his extreme left and broke thro' our line, but were met at one point by Hill's division with a loss to him of 450 prisoners; and on the extreme right by Hampton's Cavalry with a loss of five hundred prisoners. The enemy were driven back and our lines recovered. The total loss of the enemy has therefore been about fourteen hundred prisoners, and perhaps eleven hundred killed and wounded. Our loss will probably reach one-half that, say ten or twelve hundred, but even this disparity will ultimately ruin us, unless we can open up new resources of men. There is no help, I fear, except to use negroes, giving them their freedom. The common sentiment of the country is rapidly verging to this point. Judge Campbell[34] thinks it would be the knell of Slavery as it exists, but I do not see that that necessarily follows. Nevertheless the country is prepared to throw Slavery into the purchase of our independence if that be necessary to achieve it. The opening wedge to this use of Slaves is found in law of last Congress conscribing twenty thousand for cooks, teamsters, etc. The next thing will be to put them in as soldiers, giving them their freedom.—The news from West Virginia is favorable, the enemy having been driven back to Jonesboro and repulsed at another point. Early sends word to the Command-

COLONEL JOHN WILLIAM MALLET, F. R. S.
Superintendent of Confederate Ordnance Laboratories

Courtesy The University of Texas

ing Officer at Lynchburg that if the citizens will defend themselves against raiders he will look after Sheridan. Thus affairs are brightening in those directions. The loss of Fort Harrison is serious but not irreparable.—The President is on his way back from Hood's Army.

October 4th. The news from Western Virginia is that our troops whipped the enemy coming from Kentucky at Saltville, and are pursuing them. Our forces were composed entirely of reserves and detailed men, armed for the occasion. The enemy had six thousand men. Early holds the enemy in check in the Valley, and is even forcing him back. Kershaw's Division is on its way back, and is much wanted here. I attribute the partial successes of the enemy to its absence. The accounts from Missouri are encouraging. Price at the head of a large force is advancing upon St. Louis and was at last accounts at Pilot Knob, some thirty or forty miles from the city.

October 6th. Our poor harrowed and overworked soldiers are getting worn out with the campaign. They see nothing before them but certain death, and have, I fear, fallen into a sort of hopelessness, and are dispirited. Certain it is that they do not fight as they fought at the Wilderness and Spotsylvania. The cure for this is I think to *limit the term of service.* They are now in for the War, and as there appears no end to it, at present, they begin to look upon themselves as doomed men. A term of service for five years would perhaps correct this without imperiling the existence of the Army. Under such a term the men would begin to go home in the middle of 1866, but most of them in '67, and there would be constantly veterans enough to keep up the quality of the Army. This, with a proper employment of Slaves as cooks, teamsters, and even as guards and soldiers, would greatly relieve the burdens of the war on the white population.—Willie is still at Mr. Seddon's, so pleased that he don't want to come home, I fear.

October 8th. Yesterday morning our troops attacked the enemy between the Darbytown and Charles City road, and drove them out of their works, capturing ten pieces of artillery with all the caissons, and a hundred horses. The attack was, however, less decisive than was expected. The object was to pierce the enemy's line and isolate the 10th (Burney's)[35] Corps, and destroy it. It is partly composed of negro troops. The brave General Gregg,[36] of Texas, fell at the head of his troops; General Bratton[37] of S. C. severely wounded. Colonel Haskell,[38] artillery, mortally wounded. He is one of four brothers of whom two have now fallen, and one lost an arm.—Willie came back yesterday highly delighted with his visit to Mr. Seddon's place, where he had plenty of playmates.—The weather has turned suddenly cool this morning, with a bright sun, however. Hood is now in position across the Georgia Railroad, and Sherman must fight, or evacuate all his conquests. Forrest was said to be marching on Altoona, tho' he was last expected by the enemy at Huntsville.

October 11th. No news from Hood. What is Sherman waiting for? His provisions must be nearly out, and his horses pretty well starved. Will he march out and fall upon Hood, or will he perhaps form a moveable column and strike across the country for Charleston.—Our situation here is getting very critical. We have no men. General Lee's Army is reduced to about thirty thousand Infantry and say ten thousand cavalry and artillery. Grant is being reinforced daily to the extent of one thousand per day, so Colonel Chilton[39] says. He told me that General Lee said: "If we can't get the men, all that is left for us is to make peace on the best terms we can." I cannot think he was serious, but I regret to hear such language from his mouth. I heard almost the same expression now attributed to him uttered by him in June, 1861. He must be subject to fits of despondence. Our brave President never wavers thus, in act or thought.

October 16th. On Thursday the enemy attacked our line between the Darbytown and Charles City Roads, and were repulsed with heavy loss. It is ascertained that in retaliation for our placing negro prisoners at work on fortifications the enemy have put our officers and men at work on Butler's Canal. The news from the Valley is that Early attacked Crook's command and drove it back, with loss; Sheridan having detached two of his corps to rejoin Grant. —From Georgia it appears that Hood has withdrawn from his position on the Railroad, and intends moving either up the road towards Dalton, or if Sherman follows to strike over to Huntsville and up toward Nashville, thus compelling Sherman to return into Tennessee to cover Nashville.—The President made a very *awkward* speech at Macon on his way to the Army, which creates a great deal of comment. It was a very unfortunate speech to say the least of it. It seems probable that the naval prisoners, after having been brought to Varina for exchange were, at the instance of Butler, sent back to Old Point, so that poor Dick has not reached here as we hoped he would.—Willie had a little fever yesterday and today; nothing serious I hope. The death of poor little Gayle makes us anxious about him.

October 22nd. Early was again whipped on the 19th with the loss of 23 pieces of artillery. This makes about eighty pieces that he has lost since May 6th. It is time to let him retire! It seems he attacked the enemy's camp early, and surprised two corps, routing them and capturing thirteen hundred prisoners, with nineteen pieces of artillery. He pursued them until they rallied and turned upon him and attacked him in line. Then comes the old story; our left gave way; a total rout ensued, the men behaving disgracefully and scattering into the woods. The prisoners were recovered, however, It is really ludicrous this business in the Valley.

October 23rd. Dick reached here on Tuesday evening looking a good deal the worse for his year's imprisonment at Fort Warren. About 120 Naval officers returned with him. Hood appears to be striking out for Tennessee and when last heard from was at Gadsden, on the Coosa. I fear his campaign will not effect its object, and that his army will be disorganized in the attempt to draw Sherman back into Tennessee.

October 28th. There was fighting yesterday on both ends of the lines. On our left the enemy attacked at two points— between the Power House and the Charles City Road and on the Williamsburgh Road, and was repulsed losing seven colors and four hundred prisoners. On our right the enemy drive back our cavalry, but was afterwards assaulted by Mahone and Hampton, and driven to their original lines, with some loss. Our losses slight on this side—heavier probably on the south side. One of General Hampton's sons is reported killed, the other wounded.[40]—No news from Hood who has not been heard from since the 22nd.—Mary had a little daughter on Tuesday—both well—the birth somewhat premature.—Hugh commanded his brigade in yesterday's fight, and earned the commendation of General Hampton.

October 30th. General Lee telegraphs that General Hampton drove the enemy across Rowanty Creek and re-established our lines. So that in the several attacks of Thursday he has gained no ground, and has lost in killed, wounded and missing not less than 2500 men. Our loss from all causes will scarcely reach five hundred. No news from Hood yet. Forrest advises from the interior of West Tennessee that Rousseau[41] has left his quartermaster and commissary trains, taken all his infantry and hastened toward Huntsville. As soon as he can cross the Tennessee he will advance rapidly on Nashville. Will he and Hood unite to attack that point?

November 3rd. A little boy was born to us at fifteen minutes before six this evening (Thursday). Mother and son doing very well, but these are events involving terrible suffering. I hope it may be the last. Two boys and four girls in a family will do very well. May heaven bless and protect them all and bring them safely to years of maturity. It is a wet miserable evening, and as I sit writing by the blaze of a cheerful wood fire, I sorrow over our soldiers exposed to the slow, cold, penetrating rain. Heaven watch over them too.—No farther news from Hood. I fear Price has met with bad luck in Missouri, but as our accounts come wholly thro' Federal sources little reliance is to be placed on them.

November 6th. Mamma and the youngster are both doing well. I heartily wish he were a year old. Mrs. Jones stays constantly with Mamma.—Nothing of an exciting nature going on at the front. No news from Hood.—A paper of the 2nd in the War Department, states that gold is 260 and that Governor Seymour[42] has called out the militia in New York to protect the ballot box. Deserters and prisoners coming in say that there is good news for us in Missouri.

November 8th. Active operations were expected on our right yesterday and today, but the bad weather, or other causes, prevented, no doubt. It is said that many of the enemy's troops have gone home to vote. Today is their presidential election and by this time it is settled who is to be their President for the next four years. Lincoln will, no doubt, be re-elected over McClellan.—In East Tennessee our troops under General Vaughn[43] have been defeated, losing five guns. Early is reorganizing his troops at New Market. From Hood there is nothing definite tho' he appears to have crossed the Tennessee at Gunter's Landing and, perhaps, near Tuscumbia. Price does not seem to have been seriously defeated tho' he has withdrawn to S. W. Missouri about Carthage. Whether the enemy is to attack at Wilmington does not yet seem to be determined.—The loss of the "Albemarle" at Plymouth loses to us the Eastern part of

North Carolina, and the blood shed at Plymouth in the spring was in vain.

November 17th. No military operations of especial interest have occurred. Breckinridge defeated the enemy at Bull's Gap on the 14th with the loss of six pieces of artillery, ten stands of colors, two hundred prisoners, fifty wagons, etc. Sherman is said to have returned to Atlanta with four corps. With the five he has now in hand he is capable of marching on Savannah and Charleston, and capturing both places, holding them and Augusta, thus cutting us in two again.—Lincoln has been re-elected President of the United States by overwhelming majorities. There is no use in disguising the fact that our subjugation is popular at the North, and that the War must go until this hope is crushed out and replaced by desire for peace at any cost.

Sunday, November 20th. Definite news was received yesterday that Sherman had left Atlanta and was marching on Macon with 35,000 men, including Kilpatrick's cavalry. Today we learn that the enemy's cavalry were yesterday at Clinton twelve miles or so from Macon, and that a corps had advanced toward Augusta as far as Madison, some sixty miles from Atlanta. It is said to be Slocum's[44] Corps. Rains[45] is moving stores to Columbia from A. [Augusta]—Hardee has been sent to Macon. There are about five or six thousand Reserves, and Georgia Militia and Wheeler's Cavalry, say 3500 men, between the enemy and Macon. On the other route there is no force to oppose the progress of the enemy to Augusta, where I hope, however, some force will have been assembled by the time the enemy appears before it. The Secretary looks very much disturbed. I cannot learn that any provision had been made against such a movement tho' the probability has been evident for some time past. I fear the President is no military genius, tho' genius avails not much without resources. I hope the roads and the distances will destroy Sherman if the Military don't. The steamers (war) "Tallahassee' and

"Chickamauga" are both returned to Wilmington after very brief cruises (ten to fifteen days). The Navy is decidedly out of luck.—Mr. Mallory lacks earnestness and devotion to his duty. He is too good company and too generally informed to be worth much at any one thing, tho' a man of undoubted ability. He beats the Secretary of War in every discussion that arises—is in fact too smart for Mr. Seddon.

November 21st. The enemy were yesterday evening at Oconee River; and fighting was reported near Macon with cavalry of the main columns, no doubt. The impression appears to be that the troops of the enemy will combine on Augusta. General Beauregard is still at Florence, or rather the army is. What a decrepit movement that has been! If Sherman's columns are properly met the movement must end a disaster to him. I cannot see why a division is not sent down to Augusta from here. Perhaps it has been tho' I fear not. Hardee directed Wheeler to attack the enemy's cavalry at Clinton yesterday to develop their intentions.— Vice President Stephens published a letter to Senator Semmes[46] defining his views, and declaring that the Union as it was is so dead that no hand save that which raised Lazarus from the tomb could resuscitate it! This is very well, and will reassure those who thought eminent Georgians were going astray.—Mamma and baby are getting on well. Sister Mary has lost her poor little baby, two weeks old. The weather is very bad, with continued rain, which, if it extends to Georgia, will be one of our best allies.

November 24th. The column of Sherman's Army (left wing) marching on the Georgia Railroad turned south at Madison and appears to have gone to Milledgeville. The Cavalry of the other column was attacked by Wheeler at Clinton, but without gaining any advantage. Hardee has gone with the troops from Macon toward Savannah. He does not know exactly where the enemy is.—Dick came here on Tuesday. He will probably leave in a day or two for Wilmington. I was confirmed a Brigadier General by the

Senate on Saturday.⁴⁷ I owe my promotion to the President himself. Mr. Frank Lyon wrote him a note on the subject, which he endorsed over to the Secretary of War, directing the promotion.⁴⁸

November 26th. General Bragg telegraphs that the enemy was met in force yesterday at Buffalo Creek, near Sandersville. He has thus made very fair progress—nearly half the way to Savannah in twelve days from Atlanta. Wheeler with his cavalry is ordered to obstruct him in every way—hang upon his flanks and destroy everything eatable in front of him. I trust he will yet have a difficult path to traverse in getting to the seacoast.—The prisoners (Yankees) confined at Salisbury, ran yesterday and killed two of the guard. They were immediately fired upon with musketry and artillery and forty to fifty killed.

November 28th. The news last evening was that the enemy had struck the Railroad between Millen and Augusta at Briar Creek, severing communications with the front from Augusta, where Bragg is. General Wheeler confronts the infantry of the enemy at Sandersville. Lt. General Taylor was ordered to bring all his forces from Macon to Savannah via Albany, and Thomasville, the interval between these two places being a land march. Little confidence felt in the ability of General Bragg to cope with this movement. There are say five thousand troops at Macon, six thousand at Augusta, 7500 under Wheeler and the garrisons of Charleston and Savannah. Of course many of them are Reserves.

November 30th. General Bragg telegraphs that Wheeler, leaving a force to confront the enemy near Sandersville, followed the party which cut the road at Briar Creek, and attacked him at Wadesboro, gaining some advantages. Fighting was going on. It is hardly possible to divine Sherman's intentions. Bragg fears he may cross the Savannah and go to Beaufort, and adds that it is "entirely practicable." No doubt. I wish he were there and all our cities safe. We can rebuild the railroads destroyed on this extraordinary career thro' Georgia; and if he thinks the possession of the sea coast at Beaufort a compensation for the giving up of Atlanta—a place he fought so hard to gain—he is the best judge of his bargain. I fear he will turn upon Macon and Columbus, and resume his position on the Chattahoochie, say at Marietta. Still if he had an object worthy the risks he runs it must be the possession of the two lines of communication between the Northern and Southern States, say at Branchville and Pocotaligo. This would involve the fall of Charleston and probably Savannah and Augusta. We shall soon see. I doubt whether Sherman sees his way quite clearly, and hope disaster is before him.

December 2nd. The enemy appears to be not far from Millen, and has apparently met with little obstruction thus far. He is inflicting much individual misery, burning and destroying homes, crops, cotton, gins and implements, but the military results are comparatively small. At Augusta they are still doubtful of the direction of Sherman's march. It is to be hoped he will meet with more determined opposition after he leaves the Savannah.—Hood is approaching Nashville, or rather appears to be bearing toward East Tennessee—perhaps to effect a junction with Breckinridge, and march into Kentucky.

December 7th. Nothing of much interest has occurred on the lines here. The monitors come up to the obstructions occasionally and open fire on Battery Dantzler, and are replied to. The distance, 2400 yards, is too great to do much execution on them.—General Archibald Gracie was killed on Friday last, by a shrapnel. His neck was cut and dislocated by a fragment and three balls struck him in his shoulder.—A fight took place at Grahamville, between forces from the fleet and our Georgia militia, on Wednesday, in which the enemy were repulsed with considerable loss. On Monday Sherman is reported as marching down both sides of the Ogechee [sic], with four corps.

December 11th. Hood appears to have attacked the enemy at Franklin (seventeen miles from N.) on the 1st, with success perhaps, but with heavy loss. The enemy report Generals Adams and Gist[49] killed. He is now before Nashville. We hear no later news direct from Hood than the 27th, at which time he was at Columbia, the enemy retiring before him. We have probably not sufficient force to effect much against the troops of Thomas, entrenched in Nashville. Besides Steele from Arkansas and Smith from Missouri are hastening to join him.

On the 9th Beauregard telegraphs from Savannah that the enemy is approaching on the River Road, the middle ground road, and the Central Railroad, skirmishing going on. Wheeler despatches to Bragg on the 8th that he is pressing the rear of the enemy who is obstructing the roads. He says the 14th Corps is marching on the River Road; the 15th on the Middle Road and the 17th and 30th on the Railroad. Very few west of the Ogechee [sic].—Yesterday Longstreet made an attack on the enemy on the Darbytown road, results not yet known.—Hampton telegraphs that he drove the cavalry of the enemy back upon the infantry of the Corps marching South by the Jerusalem Road, and saved the Mechanics River Bridge.

Our force in front of this city is now about as follows: Longstreet's, Hill's and Anderson's Corps, with two Divisions of Early's, 44,500 infantry; Ewell's command of infantry, cavalry and artillery, 6,700; artillery of General Lee's Army 3,000; cavalry of General Lee, under Hampton 7,500; total 61,700. The infantry count is taken from the return of arms in the hands of troops, and is, therefore, reliable. I am surprised to learn that there are only seven thousand men at Savannah. I fear the place will fall and the garrison be captured, tho' Hardee talks bravely and believes he can defend it. Wheeler is behind with seven or

eight thousand cavalry, tho' how he got *behind* I am at a
loss to tell, as he was in front at Louisville with his main
force. Should Sherman receive a check at Savannah it will
go hard with his army. His Northern friends are as anxious
about him as we are about Hood.—Lincoln's message
spawns nothing but subjugation. He says the door of re-
conciliation is not yet closed, and we may lay down our
arms and return to the fold. I hope six months hence a different story will be popular at the North, especially should
we catch Sherman tripping [napping?].

December 15th. A despatch from Hood says that he
drove the enemy from their breastworks at Franklin, on
the 30th, capturing several colors, and a thousand prisoners.
His losses in Generals are enormous.—Cleburne, Williams,
Adams, Strahl and Gist[50] killed, six wounded and one captured. It is fearful and our loss in killed and wounded, tho'
he says out of proportion to the Generals must be depress-
ingly great. He gives no estimate—a bad sign.—Fort Mc-
Allister, on the Ogechee [*sic*], one of the outworks of Savannah was "carried by storm"—not much of a storm I suspect,
however. The garrison was only 150 men. Troops are still
moving down from the Valley. I think still that my notions
were correct at the outset of Sherman's movement, when I
advocated the detachment of ten thousand men to Georgia,
even at the risk of losing Petersburgh and the Southern
Railroad. It would have ruined Sherman, and with his ruin,
gone far to make the North tired of the War. What can be
the object of moving down troops now I cannot see. It is
too late—the golden moment for action in Georgia has
passed by.—A raid toward Abingdon and the Salt Works
creates some alarm.—Chattanooga and all of the enemy's
posts in East Tennessee, and North Georgia, are reported
evacuated. If we can recover East Tennessee and North
Georgia we shall have done well.

December 18th. Sherman is probably in possession of
Savannah. One of our ironclads has been captured and the

other cut off, so that we have lost command of the River. The Navy is always foremost in misfortune.—General Joe Johnston came to see me last evening. He is looking very well and complimented the condition of my department. He spoke feelingly of the loss of Generals lately at Franklin.— There is a speck of War between the United States and England in the present aspect of their relations. Seward's insulting letter to Lord Wharncliffe, in reply to the proffer of aid to our prisoners in Yankeeland; the notice to terminate the reciprocity treaty; the order of General Dix to pursue and kill raiders in future upon British territory; the resolution to build six gunboats, combined; all with Willis' [?] Brazil letter,[51] look very ominous. Yet it all may come to nothing. Let us continue to rely on our good right arms.—Baby was christened Sunday before last, two weeks ago.—The fight at Grahamsville turns out to have been a bloody one to the enemy as they confess near a thousand killed and wounded.—At Griswoldsville, near Macon, we met with bloody loss, over six hundred killed and wounded, nearly all Reserves.

December 19th. This is a gloomy day here—one of the gloomiest in our struggle. The news from Hood, thro' Northern papers asserts that he was defeated before Nashville on the 15th and 16th, with heavy loss and is in full retreat. If so his army will be nearly destroyed before he can reach a place of security. This army defeated and demoralized, there is no force to cover Alabama and Georgia, and the enemy may penetrate these states at his leisure. The plan of campaign which has terminated so disastrously is due probably to Beauregard, whose favorite plan has, it is understood, been always to enter Kentucky and carry the war to the Ohio. — Savannah cannot probably be held against Sherman.

December 20th. Savannah appears to be yet uncaptured, notwithstanding the loss of our gunboats. The news from Hood, thro' Yankee sources, continues to be unfavorable, and they say he is retreating after great losses of men and material.—Troops are moving toward Wilmington from here, and a heavy armament has departed from Hampton Roads supposed to be destined to the attack of that place. The great trouble to be met now is to feed the army here while the railroads southward are being repaired, which will take from six weeks to two months, no doubt, tho' partial communication is already re-established.

December 26th. A despondent Christmas has just passed, yet people contrived to eat hearty and good Christmas dinners. The soldiers unfortunately have not even meat, and have had none for several days. The Commissary General[52] has signally failed in his duties; while there is plenty of food in Georgia there is none here. There is no sufficient excuse for this. The food must be brought here, and the means to do so provided and organized.

Savannah was evacuated on Wednesday or Thursday. All the armament and much material lost. My Officer telegraphs that he saved nothing but his arms and ammunition. I presume our prisoners were lost. It is a sad [?] denouement to such laborious preparations. For nearly four years has it been prepared for a defence which lasted about four days. The key to the situation, Fort McAllister, seems to have been taken by surprise, thus establishing communication with the fleet of the enemy. The Yankees claim the capture of sixty pieces of artillery from Hood, and I fear it is but too true. I hope to hear, however, that he has escaped with twenty thousand men, as the nucleus for a new army.

December 27th. Savannah appears to have been evacuated on the night of the 20th (Tuesday), the last troops crossing the river about 5 A.M. of the 21st. Hood is reported by the Yankees to have lost 17,000 men, and sixty pieces of artillery since he entered Tenn. The probability is that he has lost about ten thousand killed, wounded and captured, and that he will recross the Tenn. with 20,000 men besides his cavalry. Army enough to cover Alabama and Northern Ga., if properly disciplined and led. There is deep feeling in Congress at the conduct of our military affairs. They demand that Gen. Lee shall be made Generalissimo to command all our armies—not constructively and "under the President"—but shall have full control of all military operations and be held responsible for them. This Tenn. campaign although the President can hardly be called responsible for it, except that he *suffered* it, has completely upset the little confidence left in the President's ability to conduct campaigns—a criticism I fear I have made long ago. Fort Fisher was attacked by the Porter Fleet on the 24th and again on the 25th without much effect. Troops were also landed above and assaulted, but were repulsed. The Federal fleet is about sixty vessels.

December 28th. Gen. Bragg advises that the enemy re-embarked and desists from the attack on Fort Fisher which has suffered very little damage from the heavy bombardment. Mosby was badly wounded last week. He is a great favorite and everyone asks about him with interest. It is hoped he will soon recover. S. D. Lee advises Beauregard that he will be at Okolona in a few days and wants his (B's) views on recent events in Tenn. I saw the President today and conversed with him for half an hour, chiefly on business. He remarked "I will say to you in confidence that since Bragg has gone I can get very little information of things about Richmond. (We were talking of bringing back our workmen from the trenches and replacing them with the militia). I am almost deprived of the assistance of two valuable officers by the prejudices existing against them. I mean Bragg and Pemberton. The murmurers and fault-finders will not let them alone." He said he did not think that Hood's losses would be found to be near as great as was now supposed, and that he had still strength enough to turn upon the enemy and achieve a victory. Tomorrow is the eleventh anniversary of our marriage. We will have a few friends in the evening.

Editor's Notes

1 Captain N. A. Sturdivant.

2 "Mr. Austin" has not been identified. "Mrs. Commodore Forrest" was the wife of Commodore French Forrest, C. S. N.

3 "Mrs. Captain Adams" has not been identified. "Dr. Crawford" was probably Dr. William Crawford, a brother-in-law of Gorgas.

4 Colonel John William Mallet, a British subject, was probably Gorgas's most able subordinate. Mallet was a chemist and a Fellow of the Royal Society of England. Gorgas had appointed him Superintendent of Confederate Ordnance Laboratories, and Mallet managed them with great success. Mallet turned to education after the war and ultimately became a professor of chemistry at the University of Virginia. See *DAB*, XII, 223-24. His official papers as Superintendent of Laboratories are in Chapter IV of the Confederate Records, War Records Office, National Archives, Washington, D. C.

5 These men must have been General Erastus B. Tyler of the VIII Army Corps and Colonel William H. Seward of the Ninth New York Heavy Artillery. See *B&L*, IV, 499.

6 This probably was Major Norman S. Walker, ordnance agent at Bermuda. He had returned to the Confederacy from there in late June, 1864. See *OR*, ser. I, vol. 40, pt. 2, 695.

7 "Maj. Pierson" has not been identified. The "Colonel McLean" mentioned was probably Eugene E. McLean.

8 Benjamin H. Hill. See *Jour. Congress, Confed. States*, vols. 1-7, for his career in the Confederate Senate.

9 General W. H. T. Walker was killed on July 22, 1864. See *B&L*, IV, 339. The General Smith mentioned was probably General T. B. Smith. General S. R. Gist was killed at Franklin, Tennessee. See *ibid.*, p. 453. The "Gen. Merch" mentioned was General Hugh W. Mercer.

10 George Crook.

11 This correspondence was published in the *Daily Richmond Examiner* on July 26, 1864.

12 General Joseph B. Kershaw.

13 Probably Major John Ellicott. See *OR*, ser. I, vol. 40, pt. 3, 774.

14 "Dr. McCaw" and "Dr. Spotswood" have not been identified; "Mr. Aubrey was probably Military Storekeeper William Aubrey.

[15] William H. Parker. He had commanded the C.S.S. *Beaufort*, 1861-62, and participated in the attack on the Federal blockading squadron off Charleston, South Carolina, on January 31, 1863. He commanded the C.S.S. *Patrick Henry* and *Richmond*, James River Squadron, 1863-65. See *Officers Register, Confederate Navy*, p. 147.

[16] This was First Lieutenant William B. Hall. He had served at various times on the C.S.S. *Resolute, Savannah, Huntress, Tuscaloosa, Harriet Lane, W. H. Webb* and *Missouri*. See *ibid.*, p. 79.

[17] General William F. Bartlett.

[18] General Alfred Iverson captured General George Stoneman on July 29, 1864.

[19] For a good account of the capture of the *Tennessee* and the Battle of Mobile Bay, fought on August 5, 1864, see Scharf, *History of the Confederate States Navy*, pp. 559-81.

[20] Admiral Franklin Buchanan was captured on August 5, 1864, and was exchanged in February, 1865. See *Officers Register, Confederate Navy*, p. 25.

[21] General J. J. Archer. He returned to duty on August 19, 1864. See Freeman, *R. E. Lee*, III, 496, n. 35.

[22] Generals Victor J. B. Girardey and John R. Chambliss were both killed on August 16, 1864. See Freeman, *Lee's Lieutenants*, III, 548; 594.

[23] This was John C. Pemberton, the former lieutenant-general commanding Vicksburg. He accepted a commission as lieutenant-colonel rather than not be assigned to active duty. See *DAB*, XIV, 414-15.

[24] Girardey.

[25] Gouverneur K. Warren.

[26] General Joseph Hayes was commanding the First Brigade, Second Division of the V Corps. See *OR*, ser. I, vol. 40, pt. 3, 732. For details of his capture see *ibid.*, vol. 42, pt. 1, 474.

[27] John Taylor Wood. Strangely enough, Taylor held commissions in both the Army and Navy.

[28] General Gordon Granger. For his service at Mobile see *B&L*, IV, 381; 410-12.

[29] Gayle Bayne, a son of Thomas L. Bayne.

[30] This was General J. C. C. Sanders, appointed temporary brigadier-general on June 7, 1864, and killed on August 21, 1864. See *Jour.*

Congress, Confed. States, IV, 177; and Freeman, *Lee's Lieutenants,* III, 548. Sanders' name was misspelled "Saunders" in newspaper accounts of his death.

31 Senator William E. Simms. See *Jour. Congress, Confed. States,* vols. 1-4, 6, 7.

32 General Robert E. Rodes and General Archibald C. Godwin were killed at the third Battle of Winchester, Virginia, on September 19, 1864. See *OR*, ser. I, vol. 43, pt. 1, 552.

33 Lieutenant-Colonel John Minor Maury.

34 Assistant Secretary of War John Archibald Campbell. He had been a justice of the United States Supreme Court from March, 1853, until the outbreak of the war. See *DAB*, III, 456-59.

35 General David B. Birney.

36 General John Gregg.

37 General John Bratton. He was wounded severely enough to be absent from his command from October 7 (the day he was wounded), to November 20, 1864. See *OR*, ser. I, vol. 42, pt. 1, 881-82.

38 Colonel John C. Haskell was not mortally wounded.

39 General R. H. Chilton had served as Lee's Chief of Staff until March, 1864, when he was transferred to the Adjutant and Inspector General's Department. Chilton and General Lee were always good friends after Chilton's reassignment and after the war ended. See Freeman, *R. E. Lee,* I, 641-42; *ibid.,* III, 229; *ibid.,* IV, 272.

40 Frank Preston Hampton was killed and his brother, Wade, wounded, in the action on the Boydton Plank Road, October 27, 1864. See Freeman, *Lee's Lieutenants,* III, 616; also *R. E. Lee,* IV, 514 and n.

41 Gorgas is referring to General Lovell H. Rousseau, U. S. Army, commanding the District of Tennessee.

42 Horatio Seymour.

43 General John C. Vaughn.

44 General Henry W. Slocum, commanding the XX Corps.

45 Colonel George W. Rains.

46 This may have been Thomas J. Semmes, Senator from Louisiana.

47 Gorgas was nominated for promotion to brigadier-general by the

President on November 15, 1864, and confirmed by the Senate on the 19th. See *Jour. Congress, Confed. States*, IV, 273, 275.

[48] F. S. Lyon, Representative from Alabama, wrote Davis on November 9, 1864, calling Gorgas's case to the President's attention. The President and Secretary of War, James A. Seddon, endorsed the letter favorably, and the Adjutant General was instructed to nominate Gorgas for promotion under the act of October 13, 1862. See F. S. Lyon to Jefferson Davis, House of Representatives, November 9, 1864, in Personal File of Josiah Gorgas, Old Records Section, Records of the War Department, in the National Archives, Washington, D. C.

[49] General John Adams was killed at the Battle of Franklin, Tennessee, on November 30, 1864, as was General S. R. Gist. See *B&L*, IV, 453.

[50] Patrick R. Cleburne and Otho Strahl. No General Williams was found listed as killed in accounts of the Battle of Franklin.

[51] Lord Wharncliffe was a member of the British "Committee of Organization of the Southern Independence Association," along with several members of Parliament and the House of Lords. As such, he was interested in promoting the welfare of Confederate prisoners of war. Gorgas is undoubtedly referring to a letter which Secretary of State William H. Seward wrote to Charles Francis Adams, United States Minister to England, on December 5, 1864, referring to a letter which Adams had received from Lord Wharncliffe, asking that an accredited English agent be allowed to visit the military prisons in the North with a view to allieviating the suffering of Confederate prisoners. Seward refused the permission in insulting terms. See *U. S. House Executive Document Number 1*, second session, thirty-eighth Congress, part 2, 367-68, for Seward's letter to Adams; and *ibid.*, 354-55 for Wharncliffe's letter to Adams. "Willis' Brazil letter" probably refers to a letter written by Thomas Wilson, United States Consul at Bahia, Brazil, to Antonio Joaquim da Silva Gomes, President of the Province of Bahia, on October 5, 1864. This letter protested the presence in Bahia Harbor of the Confederate Cruiser *Florida*, which Wilson claimed had no legal right to refuge. Brazilian authorities pointed out that the *Florida* was commissioned by the Confederacy, which Brazil had recognized as a belligerent power, and hence did have a right to enter the port for repairs and supplies. The exchange of correspondence culminated in the seizure of the *Florida* by the United States Steam Sloop *Wachusett*, in Bahia Harbor on October 7, 1864. Naturally, the Brazilian government was infuriated and protested violently. The *Florida* was, however, accidentally sunk before the United States government was forced to decide whether or not the ship would be restored to Brazil. For full details see *Official Records, Navies*, ser. I, vol. 3, 252-54; 269-70; and Horace Greely, *The American Conflict: A History of the Great Rebellion in the United States, 1860-'65*, II, 646.

[52] Colonel Lucius B. Northrop.

6 ★ ★ ★
The Confederacy Dies Hard

Jan. 4, 1865. Our "anniversary" evening passed off very pleasantly with a little supper and cards. Everybody is depressed and sombre. Military events have as in '62 and '63 closed against us. Still gaiety continues among the young people, and there is much marriage and giving in marriage. We were last night at a ball at Judge Campbell's, where dancing was kept up until 4 thirty in the morning. There is deep feeling in Congress relative to the situation of Mil. Affairs. Committees are investigating to determine what is to be done, and how it is that Lee's army is almost without bread and quite without meat. The Com. Gen. is trying to fasten the blame on the Sec. of War, because he would not allow provisions to be brought in and paid for on this side in cotton. I trust it will end in the ousting of the Com. Gen. He is not the man for the place which requires plain practical sense, just the sort of sense that Northrop has not.

From Charleston we hear that Sherman is crossing the Savannah in force. Troops are moving southward from here, but will I fear be too late to save Charleston. It is sad to think that after so brave a defense it is after all to be triumphed over by the foe. Hood was heard of "in the field" on the 27th, sending troops from Corinth to drive the raiders from the Mobile & Ohio R.R. I am glad to hear he is any where. It seems to be true that Price died of apoplexy —a great loss at this time.[1]

Jan. 6. No positive news of Sherman's intentions. Indications are that Charleston too will be given up—where is this to end? No money in the Treasury—no food to feed Gen. Lee's army—no troops to oppose Gen. Sherman—what does it all mean—as Judge Campbell says of the declaration of the Com. General that he cannot feed the army— what is the "significance" of it? Is the cause really hopeless? Is it to be abandoned and lost in this way? I fear as I have feared for two years past, there is no master hand at our helm. . . . I saw the President yesterday. The question was about the removal of Pemberton from the command he now holds of the Artillery defense of Richmond. He said he was about to do him an injustice in obedience to popular clamor, and wished to make it as little disagreeable to himself (the President) as possible; he desired therefore to put him on as honorable and high a duty as possible, and it was agreed to assign him to the inspection of Artillery & Ord. in the field. He agreed that Pemberton's manners were very ungracious and that he contrived to quarrel with nearly everyone he came in contact with, but thinks him a good soldier and excellent man—which I believe he is.

Jan. 10. The repulse of the enemy at Fort Fisher assumed larger proportion as the enemy's force becomes known, and it is seen how little damage they effected. Over 600 guns were brought against the works, and pounded it for two days with little effect. Hood telegraphs that his trans-Miss. troops must have furlough for 100 days. This is looked on as a bad sign of their condition. I have just returned from an examination before a committee of both houses on the "public defense."

Jan. 12. The topic of remark today is the presence here of Mr. Frank Blair Senior.[2] What his business is no one can guess, and yet everyone is wondering what it can be and why he was permitted to come here. On Sat. last a fire at Charlotte burned up 22,000 sacks of corn, 500 bales of cotton, and a variety of stores. It was accidental, but is a terrible blow in our straightened circumstances. To add to our troubles a heavy rain on Tuesday washed away a portion of the Piedmont R.R. and stopped the trains for 6 or 7 days. Gen. Lee's army has but two days food left, and an order is issued today to call on the citizens of Richmond for a part of their supplies. Willie still absent at M.H.'s.

Jan. 15. In this dark hour of our struggle there is of course strong feeling against the administration for having mismanaged our affairs. This must be expected in adversity. I have cherished and long ago expressed my conviction that the President is not endowed with military genius, but who would have done better? It is impossible to get anyone to say who, and it is probable that as much has been done with our armies as ought to be expected. The odds against us have been very great. But our finances have been badly conducted. For this the President can scarcely be held responsible. It is not a province he is expected to control. The hostility to the administration will however force some change in the cabinet no doubt. Benjamin, Mallory and Seddon are obnoxious, especially the latter. The Commissary Gen'l too, who has failed wretchedly, will be replaced I have no doubt. He has hitherto been supposed to be very partial to the President, and the President to him on account of old friendship at West Point, but this appears to have ceased, and those about Northrop abuse the President grossly, from which I infer that their principal has changed his tone. The bombardment of Fort Fisher began again on Friday—yesterday the Fort was still in good order. Blair left the city on Friday—no one appears to have learned the nature of his mission. I learn that a portion of Hood's army is ordered up to Augusta I hope, which I told the Sec. three weeks ago was the place for two corps, leaving one corps and Forrest to cover North Alabama. The force of Gen. Lee's army, including the troops under Ewell immediately about the city, is about 61,000 men (aggregate), of which 50,000 infantry, 3,500 artillery, and 7,500 cavalry. Hoke's Division, 7000, is at Wilmington, and Connor's brigade at Charleston, in addition to above. With this number of troops before us I see no cause for despondency, if we can infuse energy enough into the Coms'y Dept. to feed them.

Jan. 18. We have just come from dinner at Mr. Jones'— a party of twelve—a good dinner without wine which is getting rare. The prospect is growing darker and darker about us. On Sunday night Fort Fisher fell by assault after having repulsed the enemy until half past six; it fell at 10 o'clock by a night attack, most of the garrison being captured. A distinguished Virginian, Mr. Holcombe, tells us there is a strong disposition among members of Congress to make terms with the enemy, on the basis of the old Union, feeling that we cannot carry on the war any longer with hope of success. Wife and I sit talking of going to Mexico to live out there the remnant of our days.

Jan. 25. I have outlived my momentary depression, and feel my courage revive when I think of the brave army in front of us, sixty thousand strong. As long as Lee's army remains intact there is no cause for despondency. As long as it holds true we need not fear. The attacks of the enemy will now all be directed against that Army. Sherman from the South, Thomas from the West and Grant in front. We must sustain and strengthen this army, that is the business before us.

Old Blair has returned to this city from Washington, and is again gone. What does it all mean? Are we really to make terms with the enemy before we are half beaten? Mr. Singleton[3] has I believe gone off. His mission was more I think to see what could be made out of cotton than out of peace. Would that these birds of evil omen could be kept outside our limits. They do us no good. The Virginian legislature has requested the President to appoint Gen. Lee to the command of all our armies. He replies that he would be only too happy if Gen. Lee would undertake it, but he declines. There is a great outcry against the President, but I predict a reaction in his favor. The three ironclads went down the River yesterday. One got through the obstructions, the other stuck, and all returned. The object was to strike at the enemy's depots at City Point. Sherman is still lingering near Savannah, and making feints against the line of the Combahee. I fear he will be heard of on the right bank of the Savannah and will strike at Augusta.

Jan. 30. Old Frank Blair left last week, and on Sunday morning (yesterday) three so-called peace commissioners started off for Washington. They are Judge Campbell, Mr. Hunter and Mr. Stephens. Will anything come of it? I doubt it. They have no credentials, nor authority, but go simply to see whether anything can be agreed on, or hit on, as a basis for negotiations. Last week our flag of truce boat returning in the evening ran down one of the torpedo boats, sinking her and drowning her Commander Lieut. Armstrong.[4] The movements of Sherman are not yet determined, tho' the Augusta authorities seem satisfied they are to be the next victim of his success. Floods have destroyed they say more property and done more damage in Ga. than Sherman did on his march. Verily, we need patience and courage to fight man and Providence. Is this double affliction sent merely to assure us of our strength? I think so. I have been confined for two days with a severe cold, and today mamma is in bed with a severe neuralgia in the face, the effect of a bad cold. The weather has been very severe for four or five days past—it was milder today. A good stock of ice has been laid in.

Feb. 3. The "peace commissioners" probably reached Washington yesterday and are now pow-wowing. No one expects any results. Sherman appears to be moving up the Savannah, probably to the R.R. between Branchville and Augusta. In that case I do not see what our tactics will be, to separate by leaving a heavy force in Augusta and then get beaten in detail; or give up Augusta and unite our forces at some point near Branchville with the forces in and about Charleston. I fear Sherman has too many men for us, and will do pretty much as he pleases. Gen. Lee has

been appointed Gen.-in-chief, and Gen. Breckinridge Sec.
of War. The country continues to cry out for the reappt. of
Gen. Jos. Johnston to the command of the Army of Tenn.,
but there is nothing yet that looks that way; on the contrary, it is asserted, he is to be assigned to the command
of this Army. I trust not, for I desire to see it commanded
by one of Lee's generals, who will get inspiration from him.
Beauregard and Hardee are both at Augusta, and the two
corps ordered from Taylor's army are beginning to arrive
there. The desertions from these troops *en route* were said
to be very numerous. I hope the story is exaggerated. Our
unfortunate brother-in-law Dick has again been captured
with his vessel (the Stag) at Wilmington.[5]

Feb. 8. An attack in some force was made on our right
on Monday, our troops driven back, and Gen. Pegram
killed.[6] No great loss of men was sustained on either side,
but the enemy maintained the new position they acquired.

The road between Branchville and Augusta seems to
have been cut by the enemy somewhere about Sunday or
Monday.

The troops seem to be everywhere short of ammunition
again, and are clamoring for cartridges. The "peace commissioners" returned on Sunday, and with the answer I
expected—no terms save submission will be listened to. It
has had a good effect on the country.

Feb. 10. Yesterday there was an enthusiastic meeting on
the war, at the African Church. Mr. Hunter,[7] Mr. Benjamin and others spoke. The war feeling has blazed out
afresh in Richmond, and the spirit will I hope spread thro'
the land. Gen. Pegram was buried yesterday. Gen. Sorrel
is reported desperately wounded. The fighting of Monday
cost us some fifteen hundred. They gained a fresh position
however and held it. It is said four corps were massed
against our right. There is no doubt that a portion of
Thomas' army has been sent here. The enemy have spread
along the R.R. from the Edisto bridge, 5 miles from

Branchville to Blackville, a space of some 20 odd miles. We have a heavy force concentrated about Branchville. Col. Wood told us this evening that the President had intimated the strongest desire to Gen. Beauregard to have Charleston held, at any rate, for the present. I hope it will be done. It is of great importance to us to hold it for further supplies. The feeling against the President because he will not restore Johnston, and because he will not make the changes in the cabinet demanded by public sentiment, is growing very strong.

Feb. 16. The enemy appear to be approaching Columbia, and there is evidence from telegrams of great uneasiness there. We must expect more disaster I fear. The cup of bitterness is not yet full. Exchanges of prisoners man for man, appears to have been fully resumed. Two thousand of our men came up yesterday. This method of exchange will leave us without prisoners; if carried out to the full extent, will leave 20,000 of our men in their hands, as they are at least that number ahead of us. We have just had a little dinner party of nine, very dull. It is impossible to shake off the despondency that hangs over us. I saw Gen. Lee yesterday. He looked very much troubled and received me somewhat sternly, as I thought. The President looked pretty weak and was as kind and courteous as ever—one cannot help being pleased with him. Gen. Breckinridge carries his duties cheerfully, and will I hope make a good Secretary *because* he evidently intends to push work off upon others and not involve himself in details, which is right. I hear that Judge Campbell, Asst. Sec., may retain his position, a thing greatly to be desired. He is the mainstay of the War Dept.

Richmond, Feb. 19. On looking over my notes I find that Gen. Price is reported dead, this has since proved not to be so. I also predicted the change in the War Dept., and the Commissary. These have both come to pass. Gen. Breckinridge assumed charge of the War Dept. about the 1st of the month, and Col. St. John (Chief of N. & M. Bureau) has been made Com. Gen. with the rank of Brig. Gen.[8] It is a difficult post, but the change will save the army and perhaps the cause. We held a meeting (or rather he did) at his office last night. He invited a dozen of the principal citizens to advise him and assist with suggestions. It was a good inauguration. With Gen. Lee in command and a good Commissary Gen. we need now only vigorous measures in the dept. of finance. Congress must act by passing a good tax bill.

Charleston has been evacuated (17th) and Columbia occupied by the enemy. My losses in valuable machinery and I fear stores, have been very great, greater than ever before—perhaps than the sum of all my former losses. Why it was necessary to evacuate so hastily is not yet known. Poor Charleston! I believe however the courage of the country is really rising instead of falling; at least such is my hope from what I see and hear.

Feb. 21. The greatest consternation prevails on account of the continued advance of Sherman, who was yesterday at or near Winsboro. Beauregard fears the enemy will reach Charlotte before his troops can get there, and people join in his fears. Unless troops are detached from this army to enable Beauregard to check the advance of the enemy, I doubt whether Sherman's career can be stopped, and he will be in Virginia before many days. Possibly the condition of the roads may arrest or check him if Confederate arms cannot. Hardee's command from the lower S. Carolina, was at Florence yesterday, and ought to be at Cheraw today, thence it has three days march to Charlotte.

Feb. 23. There is no definite news of Sherman's whereabouts today. The morning papers announced that Gen. Johnston is assigned to the command of the troops in North Carolina now under Beauregard's command, he being, it is said, unfit for duty from ill health. This will at least inspire confidence if it does not lead to improvement in our

military status. Everybody is getting dumb-struck at the
rumor of the proximity [of the] evacuation of Richmond,
and mama and myself are anxiously conferring what is
best to be done—to go away or to stay. She is most inclined
to stay, with her six little children, within the enemy's lines,
and perhaps it is better than to fly one does not know
whither. Did we dream six months ago that Hood's movement to Tenn. would bring us to the pass? It is now said
that the enemy refuses to receive our prisoners at Wilmington after we had ordered them there for exchange, and will
try to capture and release them. This after a solemn engagement with Grant for an exchange!

Feb. 27. I learned with pleasure yesterday from Col.
Ould[9] that our exchanges would go on at the rate of say
2000 per day. Instead of Wilmington, Goldsboro will be the
point of delivery. Sherman's movements seem to be illy
understood. It is supposed he is moving toward Fayettes-
ville and Goldsboro. He will I hope find Hardee's, Hoke's
and Hill's forces in his way. I have strong hopes that some
harm may yet come to Sherman before he reaches a place
of safety. Here there is a good deal of consternation lest
Richmond be evacuated. An order has been given to remove
all cotton and tobacco preparatory to burning it. All the
departments have been notified to *prepare* to *move*. The
President sent for me on Saturday and expressed his uneasiness at the effect of this order on our people at home
and our prospects abroad. He thought the policy of Gen. Lee
ill-judged, and likely to have an effect contrary to that
intended, viz. to hasten legislation on the *negro bill*. He
afterwards caused the Virginia Legislature to be assured
that in no event would Richmond be evacuated. Gen. Johnston has again been assigned to command, and has assumed
charge of the troops in N.C. These when collected ought to
aggregate 30,000 men besides artillery and say 4,000 cavalry
(Wheeler's not included in the 30,000). Besides Hill is
marching with the greater part of his corps southward. He
can reach Fayetteville before Sherman can possibly get

there. Saw Mr. Benjamin yesterday—he denounces these representatives and Senators who are still hankering after peace, as "cowards and traitors." Mama is debating as to whether she with our children shall, in case of evacuation, stay in the enemy's lines.

March 2. People are almost in a state of desperation, and but too ready to give up the cause, not that there is not patriotism enough to sustain it, but that there is a senti-ment of hopelessness abroad—a feeling that all our sacri-fices tend to nothing, that our resources are wasted, in short that there is no leadership, and so they are ready to despair. It must be confessed that we are badly off for leaders both in the council and in the field. Lee is about all we have and what public confidence is left rallies around him, and he it seems to me fights without much heart in the cause. I do him wrong perhaps, but I doubt if he believes we will or can succeed in this struggle. The President has alas! lost almost every vestige of the public confidence. Had we been successful his errors and faults would have been overlooked, but adversity magnifies them. He has undoubt-edly done much, perhaps irreparable wrong, by adhering to the wrong men. Mr. Memminger ruined our finances (with the able assistance of a weak Congress), and yet the President refused to the last moment to acknowledge that Mr. M. was the wrong man. The Commissary General has brought this army to the verge of starvation, and the country to the utmost verge of ruin thereby, yet the Presi-dent has for three years kept Col. Northrop in place, tho' the whole country exclaimed against his unfitness for his duties, and the country was undoubtedly right. The Presi-dent has great qualities and shining virtues, and may yet win back the good opinion of the country in the trying times before us. We cannot lose the cause, and the President will perhaps show his strength of character in sustaining it when others have lost all hope.

We went to the wedding of Gen. St. John, our new Com-

missary Gen. on Tuesday evening (28). He married Miss
Carrington, living about 3 miles out of town. The roads
were very bad, and with a bad driver we had poor work in
getting there. There was a large company chiefly connec-
tions and old friends of the family. The bride is a most
feminine looking woman, but of decided character, and
will make a most excellent companion for him. He has won
the regard of everyone, and has the good wishes of all.
Sherman is reported moving toward Darlington and Florence, and crossed Lynch's Creek in some force at Tylers-
ville on Tuesday. He seems to be tending toward Wilmington, or perhaps some point above it on the Cape Fear
River. Johnston's order assuming command of the army
is a very appropriate one. It is a pity he was not returned
to Tupelo two months ago. That army which started last
May 60,000 is today reduced to about 12,000 disheartened
and dispirited men!

March 4. Today is the great Yankee jubilee and jubilant
are that people. I trust their crests will be brought lower
by next 4th of March. Sherman seems to be making some
progress towards Cheraw on the way to Fayetteville. I
suppose he will be able to open his way to the Cape Fear
and there get supplies. In that region of sweet potatoes
he is in no danger of starving. Were Gen. Lee to detach
20,000 men from the army it appears to me Sherman's
defeat and perhaps destruction could be accomplished before Grant could overwhelm Richmond. Mr. Singleton has
again arrived here, this time not to make peace probably
but to make money. Met last night at Baynes, Gen. Zach.
Deas just from the Army of Tenn.; Mr. Harrison, the
President's Sec.; his fiancee Miss Conny Carey; Mr. Lyon;
Mr. and Mrs. Jones, and Mr. Aubrey, four of us played
whist while the rest talked until 12. It is raining fast this
morning. We are still, as everybody is, in the greatest per-
plexity as to our future movements—to go away or to stay
is the question. The enemy threatens to advance from N.
Orleans and Vicksburg on Mobile and from Tenn. on Mid-

dle Alabama, capturing Selma and Montgomery. So there
is no assurance of safety in that direction.

March 5 (Sunday). Sheridan's cavalry moved on Staunton and our forces fell back to Waynesboro where they were
attacked and routed by the enemy on Thursday. They made
little resistance although over 1500 while the attacking
force is represented as about 5000. Our cavalry were sent
to the rear early in the winter to get forage and there was
nothing but one division of infantry (Wharton's) [10] which
had become so demoralized by defeats as to be worthless.
This lays the whole valley open and the enemy is effectually
destroying the Central and the Orange and Alex[andria]
R.R. by tearing up rails and destroying bridges. It is very
strange that Gen. Lee persists in keeping Early in command after his uniformly unsuccessful career. Rumors in
the streets give us vast victories in the Carolinas. Would
it were so. There has probably been a cavalry fight with
Kilpatrick's cavalry. If we could overcome that we might
threaten Sherman's movements and destroy his foraging
parties. We had a few gentlemen to dinner yesterday—Gen.
Deas, Mr. Aubrey, Col. Williams and Mr. Goldthwaite (Lt.).
The weather has turned sunshiny again.

March 6. The crisis of our fate is rapidly approaching,
and men's minds are harassed with doubts, fears and per-
plexity. The weak are for submission and those who have
more fortitude are affected by the fears of the timid. A few
men remain strong and if they have them conceal their
fears. Wherever three or four are gathered together there
are ominous whispers and dubious shakings of the head.
Even those whose faiths remain unshaken find it difficult
to give a reason for their faith. The Senate it is now said
are ready for *any* terms—the cowards. Pity a few could not
be taken out and hung or shot. If a soldier yields to *his* fears
in the hour of trial and is shot for it, why may not the
craven Senator be made to yield his dastardly life in the
same way? Is it less a crime, and is not his example just

as pernicious as that of the coward soldier? A few brief
months—weeks perhaps—will decide whether this cause is
to fail, and all the blood shed in it be for naught—can it be
possible? Are the names of the illustrious dead to go down
in history as traitors, instead of patriots? No definite news
of Sherman. Our forces seem to be drawing toward
Raleigh. Fayetteville, where we have an armory and an
arsenal will probably be left to its fate. Sheridan seems to
go along unmolested. He did not go to Gordonsville, but
seems to haven taken a road back toward Lynchburg.

March 9. A little good news comes today from Bragg.
The forces under him attacked the enemy near Kinston,
drove them back and captured 1500 prisoners and 3 pieces
of artillery, without sustaining very heavy loss. Yesterday
the enemy were reported across the James River, and on
the southside R.R. 25 miles this side of Lynchburg. This is
ascertained to be untrue, none having crossed the River,
but he is approaching Lynchburg and will no doubt try to
take it. I hope we shall repulse him but our troops have
fought so badly of late, that we cannot predict anything
with much confidence. Gen. Johnston is at Fayetteville
which was however being evacuated yesterday, so that we
have lost the armory and arsenal there. There are also 8
cotton factories. We heard today the reported death of
Hugh. There is still a hope it may not be true—a faint hope.
It was said he was killed in a skirmish near Cheraw. I went
to the market this morning. There was but one turkey
visible and that held at $140. Veal was selling at $10 per
lb. and none at that.

March 11. The fast yesterday was generally observed,
and many good sermons were preached—no doubt with
effect. They are needed to strengthen the failing faith of
the people. There is a little additional good news today.
Gen. Hampton attacked Kilpatrick's camp yesterday morning took his wagons and artillery and captured some prisoners, and recaptured many that he held. Is this the last

gleam of an expiring cause; or is it the dawn of its [illegible] from the night which has shrouded it? We had definite news of the death of Hugh. I saw Major Stokes,[11] Adjt. Gen. of Law's cavalry brigade, who saw him buried, and was not far off when he was killed. It occurred on the road to Cheraw from Chesterfield, about 14 miles from the former place. The enemy was reported in front, skirmishers thrown out and Hugh with a group of others rode out in front of the line of skirmishers. A volley was fired into this group from an ambush and four fell, among them Hugh, hit the Major says (on hearsay) by nine balls. The body was taken along, placed in a rude coffin, as were the others, and decently buried at Mount Hebron Church, 11 miles from Cheraw. The church stands in a pine wood about 300 yards back from the road—poor Mary! what a life long sorrow is there. But he died like a gallant soldier, on the soil of his native State and defending it against her foe.

March 14. After defeating Early at Waynesboro, and dispersing his force, Sheridan has been careening over the country without opposition, and has destroyed the system of Railroads north of the James River so that they cannot again be repaired for this war probably. Yesterday it is reported he was crossing the James River to the Southside, whence he would doubtless proceed to join Grant's left severing the Railroads in his way. The enemy behaved pretty well at Charlottesville, not destroying the University nor committing unnecessary outrage. It is reported they shot Commodore Holliss,[12] who took to the mountains. Several well known gentlemen are missing but will doubtless turn up in due time.

March 15. Sheridan is today reported to be about 15 miles from the city with his whole force, consisting as Gen. Early declares of 8000 men, each armed with a 16-shooter and four revolvers—a moving armory truly! Some fighting has been going on today, with what success is not yet ascertained. The whole of Pickett's Division and Fitz Lee's

cavalry is after him, and he ought to be brought to bay,
but he will probably escape after having caused us damages
it will take four months to repair. From Sherman there is
nothing more authentic than that we are concentrating
about Raleigh, and that Johnston apparently proposes to
give battle. He will however I think fall back, even perhaps
behind the Roanoke. The President sent in a message to
Congress on Monday which appears to have waked them
up. He demanded a suspension of the habeas corpuses, some
gold to feed the army with, a militia law, and then they
may go home. They appear inclined to respond. A month
more and the war will be full upon us again.

March 19. Hardee resisted the advance of the enemy a
few miles south of Winnsboro [?], and foiled his advance
upon Raleigh. It may have been a heavy feint to cover his
advance upon Goldsboro where he will effect a junction
with Scofield,[13] who has 10 or 12 thousand men. Our loss in
this action (16th) is rated at 500, that of the enemy much
larger. Sheridan has joined Grant, and will doubtless soon
emerge from the left of that army and operate off our
communications. The spirit of the people appears to be
again rising, that of the army remains good. Desertions
are decreasing. Bayne and I are still discussing where we
shall move our families—mama desires to remain. Today
and yesterday large bodies of returned prisoners arrived.
The weather is beautiful and is rapidly drying up the roads,
and rendering the resumption of hostilities imminent.

March 21. On the 19th Gen. Johnston attacked the
enemy at Bentonville and drove him. He was reinforced
but still driven. Reinforced still further he attempted to
take the offensive but was readily repulsed, whereupon he
intrenched. The country was wooded and difficult. This
looks as though he were covering his march toward Goldsboro where he expects to effect a junction with the forces
of Scofield. It is scarcely probable that Johnston has
strength enough to prevent this. What will be his move-

ments after this junction remains to be seen. Rumors today of a victory over Sherman are rife, but not much credit is given to them. Lee seems entirely indisposed to send any portion of his forces to the assistance of Johnston, yet 10,000 men so detached would enable Johnston to stop and perhaps overwhelm Sherman. No one can divine the reason of this inaction of Lee's. The apprehension now is for our communications with Danville, on which our supplies depend. If these are interrupted for ten days, Lee's army cannot be fed, and it must fall back. It is a most critical situation. The confidence of the country is again rising. Stragglers from Johnston's army are said to be returning. Everything depends on his ability to meet Sherman.

March 26. Yesterday morning at 4 o'clock Johnston's [Johnson's] Divn. with a part of Hill's Corps attacked the enemy's lines on the Appomattox. They carried the curtains easily, but these men swept by redoubts which overwhelmed us with their fire and compelled a return to our lines. We captured about 700 prisoners including a Brig. Gen. (Mc-Loughlin),[14] and lost 1000 killed, wounded and missing. Col. Baldwin calls the affair a *bad failure.* We lost many valuable officers. Sherman has effected his junction with Scofield and the combined force will now doubtless march on Raleigh, or on Weldon. As Gen. Breckinridge said yesterday "something must be done soon." Either Lee must uncover his position and with Johnston fall on Sherman, or Johnston combine with Lee and together fall on Grant. We are preparing to move our goods and chattels to Danville for the present. It is in vain to predict where safety resides, and we must wait to see.

March 29. We are still discussing as to what place we shall retire to. Danville appears the most feasible, and we are packing up to go there. It grieves mama to leave our comfortable quarters here and go to a new home.

March 30. Last night at about 9 o'clock the enemy made a furious attack on our lines at Petersburg. It seems to have been an attack of artillery, chiefly. The enemy yesterday moved a heavy force out upon our right, and have apparently gained a position not far from the Southside Railroad. When he gains this road I fear the lines about Petersburg will no longer be tenable. The accounts of our attack on the enemy's lines on the Appomattox show a very unfavorable result for us. Our losses cannot have been less than 2000 in killed, wounded and missing, chiefly the last.

Winnsboro,[15] *April 30.* On the 2d of April news came in, in the morning from Gen. Lee that his lines had been assaulted and broken by the enemy, and in a few hours afterwards a second dispatch that his line could not be reestablished and that Richmond must be evacuated by 8 o'clock that night. This I learned about 1 p.m. We had been making arrangements to move to Danville on the 3d (Monday). It was now impracticable to get the family and our effects ready by that time indicated, and Amelia concluded at once to remain, and we began moving all our effects up to Maria's house. At about midnight I left her, still standing like a brave woman over the remnants of her household goods which would be moved up before the day by wagon and horse I had left for that purpose. She had with her two faithful women of the neighborhood to whom she had been kind during the winter, and Willie, who dropped off to sleep about this time. At a little after midnight Bayne and I wended our way down Cary St. to the Danville Depot. All was still and orderly on the streets. In passing one of the arsenal gates, I left the Sentinel on duty at the gate as usual, and everything promised an orderly evacuation. I had given directions that nothing in my control should be burned lest fires might be general and the innocent inhabitants suffer. At a little after 1 a.m. Monday morning the train to which the car belonged on which I was, moved off but it was 3 o'clock before we left the neighborhood of Manchester. Toward 6 o'clock in the morning, as we have since learned, the tobacco warehouse on Shockoe Slip was fired and set that part of the town on fire. About 7 a.m.

the three bridges [of the ?] Danville & Petersburg R.R. were fired and the result was the burning up of a large part of the city, extending from 14th up to 8 or 9 St. and from the Water to Franklin. It was due to our own ill-advised orders. I heard Gen. Breckinridge give orders to fire the bridges; I regret that I did not interpose, as I had heard Gen. Gilmer, Chief Engineer, express most decided opinion as to the wanton destruction of R.R. bridges. I had on Saturday addressed a letter to Gen. Ewell deprecating the destruction of tobacco in the warehouses by fire and suggesting that it might be effected as well by breaking barrels of turpentine over the top of it as it lay stored. The arsenal was fired from the Petersburg bridge, and the explosion of powder and shells must have terrified the inhabitants of that part of the city, and must have spread the fire.

We reached Danville Monday evening and were received by Major Hutter. Here we stayed until the news of the surrender of Gen. Lee made it necessary for the Government to remove still further Southward. The surrender took place on Sunday the 9th. The news of it reached Danville on Monday evening. I saw the President the same evening, and he was preparing to leave Danville. He was evidently overwhelmed by this astounding misfortune. He had sent for Gen. Cooper, myself and Col. Morton, the only Chiefs of Bureaus present. But he had no instructions to give me, and I told him I would probably receive some from the Secr. of War, who would be in the following day. He left Danville the same evening with such of the cabinet as were with him, by rail for Greensboro. We left in two ambulances about 1 p.m. on Tuesday. Our party consisted of Bayne, Capt. Aubrey, myself and three others. We stopped that night at or near Yancyville at Mr. Bow's who treated us very kindly. Next day we crossed the Haw River, at a very bad ford near Haw River Horn where the bridge had been swept away. Col. Dirk, Chief Engineer for Johnston, was then preparing to build bridges for our army. We continued on to Graham and about a mile and a half beyond

I slept in our wagon. Next morning we moved on to Judge Ruffin's and breakfasted. It had rained most of the night and the roads were very bad. Judge R's family including mostly ladies were much alarmed at the prospective approach of Sherman's army. Returning a short distance on the road to Graham we took to the left, on the old Salisbury road, and traveled to Mr. Winslow's near Carraway mountain, a somewhat picturesque country. Mr. W. was evidently no "rebel." On Friday night we stopped at the home of a widow with three grown daughters who all "dipped," i.e. chewed snuff. On Saturday night at [illegible] a horse thief had been shot the week before.

On Sunday night we stopped, after crossing the Yadkin at Stokes Ferry, at a Mr. Moose. The people all live very plainly, but still have enough to eat, and we could procure all we needed of coffee, yams, or spices, of all of which we had some. On Monday we broke one of our wagons and stopped at a blacksmith shop, 9 miles from Concord, and stayed 24 hours to repair damages. His name was also Moose. On Tuesday night we went to Pioneer Mills and the next day to Charlotte.

At Charlotte we found that the President and most of the Bureau Officers had arrived and the town was crowded with cavalry and straggling infantry. We found quarters at a hospitable Inn named Mayer Baer, who gave up his best room with two sofas and a Brussels carpet to sleep on. The good woman served our meals in the parlor and took good care of us. I have a grateful recollection of Mrs. Baer (she said the children called her boys "cubs" and laughed heartily). The total dispersion of Gen. Lee's army affected that of Gen. Johnston, and it soon became evident that no further effectual military resistance could be offered. The consequence was a military convention and armistice between Sherman on the one side and Johnston and the Sec. of War on the other. This took place at or near Hillsboro about the middle of April and caused a suspension of hostilities to be resumed after 48 hours notice by either party. The armistice was based on 7 articles the principal of which provided for the disbanding of the Confederate troops which were to be marched back to the State capitals where the arms and ammunition were to be deposited with the State government, for the recognition of existing State governments, the Supreme Court to decide in case of conflicting governments; the protection of persons and property and *general amnesty*. This latter was dictated by Gen. Sherman. Nothing was said about slavery.

The convention was sent to Washington and there instantly rejected, tho' it is understood approved by Grant. The notice of termination of Armistice took effect on Tuesday or Wednesday (25 or 26th). Meantime Lincoln had been assassinated (on Friday even. the 14th) while at the Theatre, and Seward badly if not mortally wounded.

On Wednesday at 11 o'clock we left Charlotte for this place. As I rode out of the town I met the President, booted and spurred with one of his aids, Gov. Lubbock, ready to take saddle. He was going with a large escort of cavalry by the way of Yorkville, near Abbeville (where Mrs. Davis was) and thro' upper Georgia to the Trans-Miss. All the cabinet except Mr. Trenholm who is sick were with him. Before he reaches the Miss. events will have shaped themselves. Whether I shall follow remains to be determined.

Wednesday night we stopped 16 miles from Charlotte. Thursday we forded the Catawba which was deep and floated away part of our "furniture" such as tin basin, water pail, bag of useful things, corn, etc. We drove on, after drying, and reloading to "Col. Sturgis," about 8 miles from Hay Ford, where we had crossed. This was the most forlorn looking place we had yet stopped at. Tho' owning 600 acres of land, and several slaves, and tho' the "Col." was a "public" man, not unknown to local fame, there were none of the comforts of civilized life. Nothing to eat and nothing to eat it with. But one spoon with half a handle to stir all our cups. There were three daughters, one of whom did a great deal of courting with a soldier whom she had seen for the first time that day.

On Friday night we stayed with Mr. Robt. Caldwell, 17 miles from Winnsboro, and fared sumptuously. Here there were beautiful flowers and a piano, in short, civilization, which we had left behind us at Danville. Mr. C. had been stripped of everything eatable and much of his stock, first by friend and next by foe. He would receive no pay, but we left with him a small supply of coffee. We drove here by 1 o'clock on Saturday and are comfortably *distributed*. Bayne and myself at Mary's, and Aubrey and Denegre and Jas. Aiken and Mr. Wiltz at the hotel. We had heard of the surrender of Johnston's army before we left Charlotte.

Wednesday, May 3d. The orders of Johnston and Sherman on the surrender are being published. It capitulates the whole country east of the Chattahootchie, and paroles all officers on duty within the limits of Johnston's command.

There is a strong disposition to possess themselves of all property of the Conf. Govt. on the part of the people. Augusta is ruled by a mob who have broken open all public stores, and it is said private ones. All public property has been carried off at Chester and Blackstock (the terminus of the railroad). The citizens here take whatever they can lay their hands on, and have even shown a great desire to lay violent hands on a large quantity of powder here.

Thursday, May 4. The citizens here are destroying powder in store here lest the whole town be blown up. I have suggested that some of the common powder be reserved for blasting.

We are discussing the propriety of setting out again on our progress southward and will probably leave on Saturday. I desire to set forward to Alabama, as my adopted State, before again coming under the control of the authority of the U. S. Govt. We took tea at Mrs. Jas. Aiken's last night and are to dine with Mr. Taft today.

The calamity which has fallen upon us in the total destruction of our government is of a character so over-

whelming that I am as yet unable to comprehend it. I am
as one walking in a dream, and expecting to awake. I cannot see its consequences nor shape my own course, but am
just moving along until I can see my way at some future
day. It is marvelous that a people that a month ago had
money, armies, and the attributes of a nation should today
be no more, and that we live, breathe, move, talk as before
—will it be so when the soul leaves the body behind it?

Thursday, May 11. Left Winnsboro on Saturday at 1
thirty p.m. and slept at Mrs. Lyles' 18 miles out. Mrs.
Lyles' mother is first cousin to my wife. She was there—
a talkative old lady of 64. Her husband was Wm. Hains-
worth and her own name was Moss. She is from Conn. They
reside at Sumter. Mrs. Lyles' place is called *Rat Hall.* It is
3 miles from Broad River.

Sunday morning we left at 8 thirty, crossed Broad River
on a good flat worked with a rope. A poor woman sat under
a big tree on the west side of the Ferry, with her household
goods under two old tent clothes. She was waiting here for
the body of her daughter who was drowned here some 10
days before in crossing with a skiff and the body had floated down some 14 miles before it was recovered. I gave her
$50. Conf. money—worthless to me—but which she said
would assist her. We passed thro' Newberry, inquiring the
way beyond at Mr. Jones (Lambert) having picked up on
the way and deposited at his home a limping Lieut. named
Owen, formerly residing at Charleston (son of G. W.
Owen). Newberry is a pleasant looking town with plenty
of space and shade trees about the homes. We passed on 3
miles to Judge O'Neil's mill where we crossed the Railroad
tracks and continuing on to Mr. Longshore's took the left
hand road and stopped at Mr. Benton's, 1½ miles from
the [fork?] and 9½ from Newberry. Mr. B. is a wealthy
planter, owning 6,000 acres, all of which he has accumulat-
ed by his own labor, though only 48 years old. He still had
sugar, coffee and tea—treated us most hospitably and took

no pay. On Monday (8th) we crossed the Little River and
at 15 miles from Mr. B's the Saluda at Island Ford, in a
good ferry boat, where they still charged in Confed. money.
It rained a part of the day. Reached Wyatt Aiken's at 3 ½
p.m. having driven 24 miles since 7 ½. On Tues. evening
at nearly 8 o'clock, Bayne, Denegre, Fred Gayle and Mr.
Jas. Aiken arrived. Stony Point, formerly a place of note
in the old Piedmont Stage route to N. Orleans, is a mile
from here. Three sets of stages formerly left there twice a
day, and there was a dry goods and a grocery store kept
there by old Mr. Smith, grandfather of Mrs. Aiken. Col.
Aiken has a good plantation here with excellent outhouses
and good stock. His Gin and Bin are driven by steam, and
he has good boilers for syrup. Little cotton is now being
raised in any of this region. Today Judge Crump, Asst.
Secy. of Treasy., Capt. Irwin (brother of Mrs. Elzey), and
Mr. Tidball,[16] Chief Clerk of the Navy Dept., arrived on
their way back to Richmond. From them we learn that the
last vestige of the Conf. Govt. was dissipated at Washington, Ga. The escort of the President proving wholly worthless it was dismissed, and the President left with Col. Wood,
Col. Lubbock, Col. Johnston,[17] and Mr. Thorbrown[18] (formerly in the Navy) for Florida, it is supposed. The rest of
the cabinet went off separately, Gen. Breckinridge leaving
with his two sons. The government being then utterly
destroyed, there seems to be nothing left but to give our
paroles, and remain quiet, moving in meantime toward Ala.
We shall leave in the morning probably for Washington, and
there give our paroles.

Friday, May 12. Left Stony Pt. in the morning. Stopped
at Blacksmith Shop at *the homestead* to repair something
(Bayne is always stopping at Blacksmith shops to repair
damages, due I expect to his ambitious style of going down
hill.) Drove to Abbeville. Aubrey and I went to Mr. Gus
Smith's, to whom Wyatt gave me a letter, Bayne and
Denegre to Major Bow's. Had a most comfortable room and
A. and I slept well.

Saturday. Left in good time (say 7½) drove a mile on the wrong road. Crossed the Savannah river at Moseley's Ferry and stopped at the Widow Gary's about 5 miles from the ferry. Were well entertained without charge. It would be a nice place to spend a summer month or two.

Sunday, 14th. Heard that the enemy were at Elberton in force, and crossed Broad River at Baker's Ferry, taking the road to Washington and Centerville. Met a squad of 6 Yankees whom we mistook for our own people. Bayne asked them whether there were any "Yankees" at Washington! They seemed to be quite as willing to pass us as we were to pass them. B. and I rode on to Washington while the wagons went on to Centerville. We got *paroles* for ourselves, and the two others.

Editor's Notes

[1] Sterling Price was not dead. He died on September 29, 1867. See *DAB*, XV, 216.

[2] Francis P. Blair, Sr., was in Richmond trying to bring about peace. His efforts resulted in the Hampton Roads Conference, which came to nothing. See *DAB*, II, 330-32.

[3] James Washington Singleton. He had been an agitator for peace all during the war. See *DAB*, XVII, 191.

[4] Aeneas Armstrong. He had served on the C. S. steamers *Savannah*, *Sampson*, and *Isondiga*, Savannah station, 1862-64, and on the C. S. S. *Fredericksburg*, James River Squadron, 1864-65. He was drowned on January 26, 1865, when the steam packet boat *Hornet* collided with the *Allison*. See *Officers Register, Confederate Navy*, p. 5.

[5] Richard H. Gayle was tricked into entering Wilmington with his command, the *Stag*, on January 20, 1865, and was captured. See the editor's "The Capture of a Confederate Blockade Runner: Extracts from the Journal of a Confederate Naval Officer," in *The North Carolina Historical Review*, vol. XXI, no. 2, 136-38.

[6] General John Pegram was killed in an action at Hatcher's Run, the Petersburg defenses, on February 6, 1865. See Freeman, *Lee's Lieutenants*, III, 629.

[7] R. M. T. Hunter.

8 Isaac M. St. John was made commissary-general of the Confederate Army on February 16, 1865.

9 Robert Ould.

10 General Gabriel C. Wharton.

11 Major John G. Stokes was on the staff of General Evander M. Law. See *OR*, ser. I, vol. 47, pt. 2, 1207.

12 "Commodore Holliss" may have been George N. Hollins. See *DAB*, IX, 152.

13 John M. Schofield.

14 General Napoleon B. McLaughlen, commanding the Third Brigade, First Division, IX Corps. See *OR*, ser. I, vol. 46, pt. 1, 331-32 for details of his capture during the Confederate attack on Fort Stedman.

15 Winnsboro, South Carolina.

16 William Wood Crump. Edward M. Tidball, Chief clerk in the Navy Department.

17 William Preston Johnston.

18 Charles E. Thorburn.

Bibliography

Manuscripts

Gorgas, Josiah. Personal file of Josiah Gorgas, Old Records Section, Records of the War Department, National Archives, Washington, D. C.
Huger, Benjamin. Mss. and papers of Benjamin Huger, relating to the Mexican War, in the War Records Office, National Archives.
Mallet, John William. Official papers and mss. of John William Mallet, in Confederate Records, Chapter IV, War Records Office, National Archives.
Ms. Report of a Board of Officers appointed to investigate the explosion of the Confederate Laboratory on Brown's Island, Richmond, in Confederate Records, Chapter IV, vol. 99, War Records Office, National Archives.

Newspapers

Daily Richmond Examiner, for the war years.

Printed Sources

Jones, John B., *A Rebel War Clerk's Diary,* reprint edition, New York, 1935. 2 vols.
Journal of the Congress of the Confederate States of America, 1861-1865, Washington, 1904. 7 vols.
Matthews, James M., ed., *Statutes at Large of the Confederate States . . .,* Richmond, 1862-1864.
Official Records of the Union and Confederate Navies in the War of the Rebellion, Washington, 1894-1922. 30 vols.
Register of Officers of the Confederate States Navy, 1861-1865, Washington, 1931.
Rowland, Dunbar, ed., *Jefferson Davis, Constitutionalist; His Letters, Papers and Speeches,* Jackson, Miss., 1923. 10 vols.
U. S. 38th Congress, 2nd Session, *House Executive Document 1, part 2* (U. S. 1217).
Vandiver, Frank E., ed., "The Capture of a Confederate Blockade Runner: Extracts from the Journal of a Confederate Naval Officer," in *The North Carolina Historical Review,* vol. XXI, no. 3, April, 1944.
War of the Rebellion: A Compilation of the Official Records of the Union and Confederate Armies, Washington, 1880-1901. 128 vols.

Secondary Works

Adams, James T., and Coleman, A. V., eds., *Dictionary of American History*, New York, 1940. 5 vols.

Alexander, E. P., *Military Memoirs of a Confederate*, New York, 1907.

Capers, H. D., *The Life and Times of C. G. Memminger*, Richmond, 1893.

Collins, Lewis, *History of Kentucky*, Covington, 1874. 2 vols.

Cullum, George W., *Biographical Register of the Officers and Graduates of the United States Military Academy at West Point, N. Y., From its Establishment, in 1802, to 1890 With the Early History of the United States Military Academy*, 3rd edition, Cambridge, 1891. 3 vols. and supplemental volume, 1901.

Douglas, Henry Kyd, *I Rode With Stonewall*, Chapel Hill, 1940.

Eisenschiml, Otto, *The Story of Shiloh*, Chicago, 1946.

Enyart, O. M., comp., *A Biographical Congressional Directory, 1774 to 1903*, Washington, 1903.

Freeman, Douglas Southall, *Lee's Lieutenants*, New York, 1942. 3 vols.

———, *R. E. Lee; A Biography*, New York, 1934. 4 vols.

Fuller, Claude E., and Steuart, R. D., *Firearms of the Confederacy . . .*, Huntington, W. Va., 1944.

Gorgas, Josiah, "Ordnance of the Confederacy, I," in *Army Ordnance*, XVI, Jan.-Feb., 1936.

Grant, U. S., *Personal Memoirs . . .*, New York, 1885. 2 vols.

Greeley, Horace, *The American Conflict: A History of the Great Rebellion in the United States, 1860-'65*, Hartford and Chicago, 1864-1866. 2 vols.

Henry, Robert S., *The Story of the Confederacy*, Indianapolis, 1931.

Holland, Cecil F., *Morgan and His Raiders, A Biography of the Confederate General*, New York, 1943.

Horn, Stanley F., *The Army of Tennessee*, Indianapolis and New York, 1941.

Johnson, Allen, and Malone, Dumas, eds., *Dictionary of American Biography*, New York, 1928. 20 vols. and supplement, 1944.

Johnson, R. U., and Buel, C. C., eds., *Battles and Leaders of the Civil War*, New York, 1887. 4 vols.

Johnston, R. M., and Browne, W. H., *Life of Alexander H. Stephens*, Philadelphia, 1878.

Lonn, Ella, *Salt as a Factor in the Confederacy*, New York, 1933.

Owsley, Frank L., *King Cotton Diplomacy . . .*, Chicago, 1931.

Pemberton, John C., *Pemberton, Defender of Vicksburg*, Chapel Hill, 1942.

Rhodes, C. D., *History of the Cavalry of the Army of the Potomac*, Kansas City, 1900.

Roman, Alfred, *Military Operations of General Beauregard in the War Between the States, 1861 to 1865*, New York, 1884. 2 vols.

Scharf, John T., *History of the Confederate States Navy from its Organization to the Surrender of its Last Vessel*, Albany, N. Y., 1894.

Schwab, John C., *The Confederate States of America, 1861-1865; A Financial and Industrial History of the South During the Civil War*, New York, 1901.

Index

lanta, 139; at Franklin, Tenn.,
154, 155; at Gadsden, 148; at
Lovejoy's Station, Ga., 139;
rumored death of, 63; rumored
to want Hardee relieved, 140;
on Trans-Mississippi troops,
164

Hooker, General Joseph, 25, 38,
48, 51 n7, 95, 132; defeat of,
36; replaced by Meade, 47

Hornet, steam packet, 186 n4

Housatonic, U.S.S., sinking of, 86,
117 n7

Huger, General Benjamin, 20
n25; negligence of, 8

H. L. Hunley, Confederate submarine, 117 n7

Hunter, Mr., 115

Hunter, General David, U.S.A.,
113, 115, 119 n50, 121, 122

Hunter, R. M. T., 2, 18 n8, 167,
168, 186 n7

Hunton, General Eppa, C.S.A.,
98, 101, 117 n21

Huntress, C.S.S., 160 n16

Hutter, Captain E. S. (Major),
C.S.A., 98, 117 n20

Impressment, fear of, causes
hoarding, 69

Indianola, U.S.S., capture of the,
24

Ingraham, Duncan N., 51 n5, attacks blockading squadron at
Charleston, 24-25

Irwin, Captain, 185

Isondiga, C.S.S., 186 n4

Iverson, General Alfred, C.S.A.,
131, 160 n18

Ives, Colonel J. C., aide to the
President, 106, 119 n41

Jackson, General Andrew, 106,
119 n42

Jackson, James T., 1, 17 n3

Jackson, T. J., 6, 7, 8, 11, 13, 25,
35, 39, 54 n41, 63, 69, 95; body
of, arrives in Richmond, 53
n36; gives orders to Federals,
20 n22; death of, 38, 53 n33,
rumored, 16; valley campaign
of, 5-6; wounded, 36, 37

Jenkins, General Albert G.,
C.S.A., 99, 118 n26

Jenkins, General Micah, 62, 79
n12, 97, 99

Johnson, Andrew, nominated for
Vice-president of the U. S.,
115

Johnson, General, C.S.A., 45

Johnson, General Bradley, C.S.A.,
133

Johnson, General Bushrod, C.S.A.,
178

Johnson, General Edward, C.S.A.,
102, 118 n31

Johnston, General Albert Sidney,
3; death of, 3; fights battle of
Shiloh, Tenn., 3

Johnston, General Joseph E., 1,
2, 39, 40, 42, 43, 44, 48, 50, 57,
61, 66, 73, 80 n19, 94, 97, 103,
104, 106, 107, 108, 109, 110,
114, 122, 124, 125, 128, 171,
175, 177, 178, 181; appearance
of, 156; arranges terms of surrender with W. T. Sherman,
181; assumes command of
Army of Tennessee, 173; attacks at Bentonville, N. C.,
177; commands Army of Tennessee, 74, 170; compliments
Gorgas on Ordnance Department, 156; on losses at Franklin, Tenn., 156; at Marietta,
Ga., 111; needs ammunition,
41; probable strength of army
of, 42; relieved of command,
127; rumored in Richmond,
132; sees Gorgas, 156; sentiment in favor of, 169; strength
of army of, 39; surrenders,
183; wanted as commander of
Army of Tennessee, 168;
wounded at Seven Pines, 5

Johnston, Colonel William Preston, 185, 187 n17

Jones, Mr., 88, 166, 173

Jones, I. Alfred, 126

Jones, John B., viii, 81 n24

Jones, General John M., C.S.A.,
killed, 97, 117 n18

Jones, Lambert, 184

Jones, Mrs. Mary, 29, 32, 42, 43,
52 n20, 67, 86, 88, 105, 116,
149, 173

121, 123, 124, 129, 136, 140, 146, 152, 153, 154, 157, 163, 165, 167, 168, 174, 176, 177, 179, 180, 183; during evacuation of Richmond, 179; railroads, 92; resumed with Lee's army, 102; shortage of, 66

Tredegar Iron Works, Richmond, Va., 91

"*Trent* Affair," 46

Trent, British Mail steamer, 46

Trenholm, George A., 182

Tucker, Captain J. R., 51 n5

Tuscaloosa, C.S.S., 160 n16

Twiggs, General David E., death of, 11, 20-21 n29

Two Brothers, schooner, 79 n13

Tyler, General Erastus B., U.S.A., 126, 159 n5

Tyler, Mrs. John, desires to leave Confederacy, 58

Vallandigham, Clement L., 39, 41, 44, 53 n37

Vance, General Robert B., C.S.A., 82 n40; captured, 77

Vance, Zebulon B., Governor of N. C., 82 n40

Van Dorn, General Earl, 3, 10, 24, 51 n3; death of, 37; defeated by Rosecrans, 22; Holly Springs raid of, 24; at Pea Ridge, 18-19 n11

Vaughn, General John C., C.S.A., 149, 161 n43

Venus, Confederate blockade runner, loss of, 67

Vera Cruz, Mex., 70

Vicksburg, Miss., 10-11, 27, 31, 33, 35, 38, 39, 40, 41, 42, 43, 44, 46, 49, 55, 56, 58, 83; invested by Federals, 40; munitions in, 40; surrender of, 48

Virginia, Confederate ironclad, 101

Virginia, Governor of, 75, 110

Virginia, secession of, 2

Virginia Military Institute, Cadets of, at New Market, 118 n36; receive thanks of Confederate Congress, 110, 119 n47

Volunteers, Confederate, 13

W. H. Webb, Confederate steamer, 54 n46, 160 n16

Wachusett, U.S.S., 162 n51

Walker, General James A., C.S.A., 101, 118 n29

Walker, Major Norman S., C.S.A., 126, 159 n6

Walker, General W. H. T., C.S.A., 159 n9; killed, 128

Walker, General W. S., C.S.A., 119 n44; captured, 106

Ward, John Elliott, 42, 54 n39

Warren, General Gouverneur K., U.S.A., 99, 135, 160 n25

Water Witch, U.S.S., 119 n51; capture of, 114

Weather, hampers military operations, 89

Webb, Walter Prescott, xi

Weehawken, U.S. monitor, 81 n28; loss of, 73

Welles, Gideon, U. S. Secretary of the Navy, 46

Wessels, General Henry W., U.S.A., 93, 117 n13

West, Captain, 66

West Indies, 16

Wharncliffe, Lord, 156, 162 n51

Wharton, General Gabriel C., C.S.A., 174, 187 n10

Wheeler, Joseph, 23, 32, 67, 70, 127, 128, 130, 135, 136, 138, 150, 151, 152, 154, 171

White House, Va., 47; rumored Federal landing at, 45

Whiting, General William H. C., 76, 82 n34, 103, 104; relieved, 105

Wilderness, battle of the, 98, 114

Wilkes, Charles, 46

Williams, Colonel, 43, 174

Williams, General, C.S.A., 155, 162 n50

Williams, Mrs., John H. Morgan stays at house of, 140

Williamsburg, Virginia, action at, 4

"Willis," 156, 162 n51

Willis, Colonel Edward, killed, 111, 119 n48